Dancing Heads

Dancing Heads

✦

a hand- and footbook for creative/
contemporary dance with children and
young people from 4 to 18 years

Leanore Ickstadt

iUniverse, Inc.
New York Lincoln Shanghai

Dancing Heads
a hand- and footbook for creative/contemporary dance with children and young people from 4 to 18 years

Copyright © 2007 by Leanore Ickstadt

iUniverse books may be ordered through booksellers or by contacting:

iUniverse
2021 Pine Lake Road, Suite 100
Lincoln, NE 68512
www.iuniverse.com
1-800-Authors (1-800-288-4677)

Because of the dynamic nature of the Internet, any Web addresses or links contained in this book may have changed since publication and may no longer be valid.

The views expressed in this work are solely those of the author and do not necessarily reflect the views of the publisher, and the publisher hereby disclaims any responsibility for them.

All photographs by Klaus Rabien, Berlin except for the author portrait (Ulrike Schmidt, Berlin), Girl with Soap Bubbles (photonica/Paul Vozdik) and Boys Jumping (Franz Kimmel, Munich).

ISBN: 978-0-595-47253-6 (pbk)
ISBN: 978-0-595-91529-3 (ebk)

Printed in the United States of America

Contents

Acknowledgments

When a mover becomes a writer various problems appear. I am extremely thankful to Michaela Ulich, not only for her help in solving these problems, but for her unflagging enthusiasm and support. Valuable suggestions were made by Karen Bamonte, Brenda Dixon Gottschild and Hellmut Gottschild, who were kind enough to read early drafts. This would have been a very different book without the students, teachers and teaching students at the Tanz Tangente, Berlin. The fact that the book exists at all is largely due to my husband, Heinz Ickstadt. His encouragement, belief and enthusiasm kept me dancing on the bad days and writing when I would rather have been dancing. For their understanding and support, and the readiness to cook their own dinner when necessary, my deep gratitude to our sons Markus and Mischa.

Preface

When we start to teach, we teach what our favorite teachers taught. We also tend to teach as they taught. We assume the "what" and the "how", glad to be in a safe harbor on the sea of movement. As years go on and teaching experience increases, we notice things that don't work as well: didactic practices (the "how") don't have the desired effect, the material (the "what") doesn't seem to answer the needs of our students. Trying to solve these problems should lead us back to the "why": why am I teaching dance to these people; and exactly what sort of dance am I trying to teach. All these questions take us back to the "how",—a re-examination of one's own teaching practices.

Over the years I have made several turns and swerves in the way I teach, what I teach and how and what I choreograph. Sometimes I have been stimulated by my adult students, by the children, often by the teenagers and by the teachers and professional dancers I have worked with. Very often an idea has taken root after I have thrown the book in the corner or walked out of the concert, disgusted with what has been offered as expertise. In fact these moments have often proved the most stimulating. The same is true of unsuccessful classes. "Why didn't it work?" is the hardest question to answer, and, for me, the most productive.

Dancing Heads offers an examination of the 'what', 'how' and 'why',—not just recipes with which to cook your classes—although they are also included—but an analysis of the ingredients,—solutions which hopefully will enable the teacher to design her own menu in the future. This approach can be useful to beginning dance teachers and for those with experience. It can provide guidance to schoolteachers (with a strong dance background as hobby dancers) in introducing dance as a subject in the school curriculum. For professional dancers seeking a new career in teaching it can provide the needed pedagogical framework. It cannot take the place of a solid background in dance technique.

Teaching day after day, year after year can wear out even the hardiest ideals. **Dancing Heads** re-examines the structure of a class, questioning traditional methods and suggesting new approaches. Detailed suggestions for starting a new class at various ages, introducing improvisation and composition and making dances with children and young people are offered. Ideas, structures and methodology are presented which can motivate and keep students and teachers interested in the dance classes they share, in dance studios and in public schools. Suggestions for more advanced improvisational, compositional and choreographic work are provided, as well as teaching curricula for ages 4 through 18 and suggestions for renewal when all else has failed. In addition to this, I have included scenes from a dance teacher's daily life,—"reality checks"—which describe some of the problems we all face when we teach, as well as possible solutions and an analysis of "what's going on here".

Basic Premises

A class in creative dance for children (4-9 yrs.) or contemporary dance for young people (10-18 yrs.) makes many demands on the teacher: to technical and compositional skills come the ability to work together in a group and to think independently,—teaching aims particular to this form of dance.

These specific aims should influence training, form the organization of the class,—the teacher-student relationship and the relationships between the students,—as well as fostering responsibility and respect at all levels.

Four to six year olds need to have fun, but to have fun learning. As the students grow older, the material and methods used must grow and develop with them. For this reason I make a distinction between creative dance for 4-9 year olds and contemporary dance for 10-18 year olds. Although all dance should be creative, at about 10 years the students tire of "games". They want to know what's "right" and what's "wrong", "good" and "bad", and to be able to measure their progress. If these desires are not met in the dance class, the teacher will lose students who become tired of "baby stuff". It is at this point that the teacher is most challenged. She[1] must be able to draw on extensive knowledge and experience with newer forms and structures, which can catch the students' imagination while challenging and enlarging their skills.

The teacher is not only the authority on dance itself, her values and attitude have great influence on the students' behavior to each other and their attitude toward dance. Class structures which loosen frontality, though sometimes threatening for the teacher, can lessen dependence on the teacher, encourage responsibility, strengthen students' independence of thought and judgment and foster a feeling of empowerment through ownership of the material. Although she relinquishes her authoritarian role, the teacher remains the expert, providing guiding knowledge and skills to the student.

New Dance, Ausdruckstanz, Creative Dance, Modern Dance, Expressionist Dance, Contemporary Dance,—whatever it is called,—needs creative and

---

1. For the sake of simplicity, I will refer to teachers and students in the feminine form. This is a reflection of the reality in dance schools. I welcome male teachers as readers, just as we all welcome boys in our classes (and wish there were more).

responsible practitioners, responsible to the art and craft of dance, to each other and to their audience. No matter if our students become dancers or members of that audience, it is our responsibility as teachers to answer these needs.

1

A DIFFERENT WAY OF LOOKING AT STRUCTURE

The emphasis on creativity, independence and self-reliance in creative or contemporary dance classes does not eliminate the need for structure. If we analyze the conventional, well-established class pattern—warm-up, technique, combination—three goals emerge:

> arousing consciousness (warm-up)
> strengthening (technique)
> refining/improving. (Combination)

Rather than blindly following "what we learned from our teachers", this analysis can stimulate new ideas for each phase.

For classes in creative or contemporary dance it's very easy to **arouse the consciousness** of the students. Improvisational games and structures followed by evaluation can provide spontaneous insights which emerge only after years of study in other dance forms, if at all. In addition, using a game or improvisation at the beginning of the class immediately establishes a mood of experimentation and sharing which is very different from what the students experience standing at the barre or in lines facing the mirror. In the next chapter I have provided suggestions for starting a class at various ages.

Problems start with the goal of **strengthening**. This can really only be achieved through repetition. Today's youngsters are not accustomed to repetition. Repeating an exercise week for week may make them stronger, but it will not make them happier or more enthusiastic. Classes in creative or contemporary dance can offer alternatives:

> Providing variety in space, rhythm, emphasis in one exercise from week to week will vary it somewhat (see section on technique versus creativity). It is also always important at some point to provide the reason for the technique,—why should the knees be over the feet on a plie, why bend the knees on landing from a jump,—but without putting yourself in the position of justifying your directions.

>Alternating energetic, improvisational phases with given material forces the students to move from one movement dynamic to another and provides a change of focus from "what the teacher wants" to "what I want".

> Presenting goals which are reachable over a short term motivates the students.

In addition, if we analyze traditional goals, we can apply them to creative/contemporary dance without using their forms.

> The idea of *"en Croix"*, for example, emphasizes spatial direction and mobility of the hip joint; the modern counterpart of this is the ability to move the arms or legs individually with or without a stabilized torso.
> *turnout* in the hip joints enables spirals, turns and helps in equilibrium.

Although the 90-degree turnout is definitely not a goal in modern dance, enabling a natural rotation in the hip and aligning knee and foot properly is definitely a necessary working area.

stretching the foot gives flexibility and strength. Increasing articulation is another area necessary for modern and contemporary dance.

These are very basic skills, which can be mastered without using tendues, the five positions of the feet or a formula of arm movements.

Last but not least, repetition itself, on the long or short range, provides strength and trains muscle memory.

Refining/improving is very dependent on the choices made for this part of class. If the teacher chooses improvisation, she must guide the students toward careful observation and evaluation while maintaining a non-threatening atmosphere. If she chooses to give material, to teach a combination, she must maintain the students' enthusiasm, match the technical level of the class, referring to past experiences, and at the same time offer them challenges with new material.

Finally, even if the combination is not finished and even if it is not perfect when time runs out, every class should offer the opportunity to "dance out"—whether it be in an improvisation, a combination (even in an unfinished state) or leaps at the end of class. Isn't that why we're all dancing?

Class Planning as a creative dialogue

Lesson plans are usually required during a teacher's education. The formula is given,—so many minutes of this and that, this learning goal, this time for reflection asking this sort of question—and one fulfills it as a matter of duty. It gives the observer an objective frame with which to measure the learning teacher's organizational skills. It does very little to nurture or stimulate the teacher's imagination or engagement with the students. As soon as her education is finished and she begins to teach, these formal lesson plans vanish, replaced by personal notation for combinations, lists of music to be used and any learning goals or aims the teacher may have decided to incorporate for the coming class.

Instead of a formula, planning for a lesson can be an ongoing creative process, one that extends from the first class to the last of the season or year and even beyond. The result of two dialogues, it teaches the teacher as well as the students, helping to widen her viewpoint and extend her horizons.

The first dialogue is between the teacher and herself.

It is based on her **knowledge** of what each age level brings to the class and what she should be expected to provide and how, in other words, the curriculum, and her awareness of elements of class structure,—raising the cardio-vascular rate, the necessity of improvisational work along with technique, the opportunity to dance out, the possibility for interaction between the students as well as between the students and the teacher.

These elements form the basis for her **choice** of teaching goals:

> what she wants to achieve in an individual class;
>
> in each group of students; over a longer timeframe;
>
> if a product-oriented process (performance) is necessary, advantageous and/or possible,
>
> and if it is, what sort of production to work toward.
>
> In addition to her knowledge comes her **experience**: her own notes from past classes; interaction with peers at workshops, hospitations and team teaching; her own dance training and teaching training; her own past successes and failures in the field.

All of this appears self-evident. In reality, the pressure of teaching many classes narrows down the possibilities. We tend to bounce off fewer walls, to weigh fewer alternatives. The range becomes narrower as our view of the possibilities zeroes in on the last class or the next performance. We tend to view ourselves as the lone provider of knowledge with no nourishment coming back from the classes themselves. A sample lesson plan from a book or magazine stimulates only until that lesson is given. The next class poses the same problems. Remembering the wealth of knowledge, of possibilities, indeed, of necessities help to widen the teacher's viewpoint and provide stimulus and motivation.

The second dialogue is between the teacher and her students and happens during and immediately after the class as a result of asking the following questions:

> What worked? why?
>
> Is it possible/advantageous to repeat? Is there another approach?
>
> and its corollary: What didn't work? why?
>
> Is it possible/advantageous to repeat? Is there another approach?

What did you miss in class?

> Was there too much music? not enough concentration?
> no time for reflection? no chance to dance out?

What did the students miss in class?
Did they request anything?
Did you promise anything?
What variations from the plan occurred?

> Why?

How did the changes or non-changes affect the class as a whole?

These evaluations made during or immediately after the class need not be long. My notebooks are filled with laconic notes like "didn't", "Oooops—try again", "awful" "great! Don't repeat!" It doesn't take long to scribble these comments down as the class is leaving, or before the next one arrives. They help to recall the class situation when you are planning the next class, providing ideas and stimulation and, incidentally, continuity.

After a vacation or a pause, it also helps to review all the available sources,—curriculum, class notes and reactions—to formulate new areas to emphasize for the class or classes you teach. Even if these lists only serve to prime the pump, to get you back into the feeling of teaching these students, they are a tangible help. They can provide a reference point to check your progress, and a reminder of areas that need to be worked on in the future.

A dialogue presupposes the ability to listen, to be aware of what your partner is saying and respond to it. In this case, a dialogue can only emerge when the teacher is aware of the signals coming from the class. Whether it's an inability to perform a given movement sequence, a misunderstanding about the theme of an improvisation or a group dynamics problem, it is the teacher's responsibility to respond to what is happening in the class. Sticking doggedly to a plan, no matter what occurs, is not only counter-productive; it sometimes can be downright impossible. Being open to the reactions of the students,—their facial expressions (can they look you and each other in the eye? are they interested?), their physical language (are they backing off into a corner? looking at the clock? losing energy, slumped shoulders, leaning on the barre or the furniture)—can help you avoid the cliff before the class falls into the precipice. Experience helps. It's very hard for a very new teacher to keep her mind on anything but her plan. How many brushes had she planned? Where's the one in the music? Has she spent too much time on floor exercises? It is hard to watch the class too. One becomes very self-involved. The trick is not to stay that way. Watch your students and listen to them. They are quite wonderful. They will give you all kinds of help if you let them.

Developing Technical Skills: Technique vs. Creativity

Like everything else in a creative/contemporary dance class, the question of technique,—if and how it is taught—depends very much on the individual teacher. For me, technique is the key to a broader movement vocabulary. No matter how imaginative a dancer is, if the body can't respond, all the ideas in the world cannot help. So, let's simply assume that we grant technique its value in a creative dance class. The problem arises: what to teach and how.

I was once asked by a pedagogy student with a strong background in classical ballet, exactly what one was supposed to teach in creative and contemporary dance. The lack of a codified movement vocabulary seemed confusing to her compared to the strict definitions of classical ballet.[1]

If the elements of self-determination and independence of thought, which I mentioned in the introduction, are factored in with an apparent lack of recognizable technique, a class in creative or contemporary dance could, for a parent, seem an impenetrable stew of scarf-waving anarchy. (It is for this reason that many parents send their children to ballet class—you know what you get, and it's been there for hundreds of years.)

Technique is the tool that enables the dancer to move his/her body through time and space according to the dancer's, the choreographer's or the teacher's wishes, no matter what the style or school. In creative/contemporary dance it should remain basic without imposing a style of movement on the student.

For a teacher

> It provides the one time in the class for consciously building strength.
> It schools memory,—musical and muscle memory and incidentally provides an objective measure for progress.

---

1. Some forms of modern dance have become codified too. Graham and Cunningham technique, although very different from each other, are both codified in the movements that are taught in classes and used in the choreographic work. The Limon technique is easily identified even in its varied forms. In addition there are the many release techniques and kinds of body work which have become a popular addition to professional dancers' training. As dancers begin teaching, these techniques find their way into classes for children and young people.

For a student, however, technique is often the most boring part of class:

> > one stands or sits in one place;
> > the exercises repeat, in themselves and from class to class;
> > the exercises are difficult ("my leg doesn't go up that high")
> > or painful ("I can't reach my toes");
> > it seems to have nothing to do with "dancing".

"But we did this last week!"

Repetition is necessary to develop strength. Most dancers enjoy this repetition. Children and young people do not. Although it is necessary to structure all technical exercises rhythmically and spatially, creative and contemporary dance offer more possibilities for variety than most other dance styles and forms.

> > Changing fronts during an exercise for body or legs swings makes the exercise completely different for the student. It also develops spatial awareness, so necessary for contemporary dance.

> > Inserting an improvisation phase of 8 counts during a foot exercise not only loosens the students' bodies (incidentally reminding them that there's more than just the feet to worry about). It reminds them of musical phrases, presents the necessity of changing the focus of concentration, and gives them a chance to 'do their own thing'.

> > Changing the music used for technique exercises on a regular basis and using a different movement quality (dynamic) can transform a technical exercise. Varied dynamics within an exercise make it seem more like "dancing".

> > Working facing a partner can eliminate the "zombie" faces we are treated to when the students face away from the mirror.

> > Having one youngster assist another increases concentration and involves them in the teaching process. Role-playing is always fun.

> > Dividing the class into smaller groups which do the exercise one after another, remaining in the meter, schools musicality and maintains concentration, at the same time allowing the teacher to observe individuals.

Establishing standards

The most important elements in choosing or developing technical exercises are

Is it healthy, helping to develop the body in a way that prevents injury?

Splits, bridges, arabesques, stretching the leg on the barre are just a few of the surprises a teacher can find when the students enter the space before she arrives. Although it takes a lot to injure a young body, it is the duty of the teacher to emphasize from the beginning the importance of warming up and preparing for these extreme movements (which they have usually picked up from friends who take other dance classes). Exercises, which might endanger knees, hips and spines, should be avoided.

Does it provide challenge in achievable increments and in specific areas?

If the students are hopelessly over-challenged, they will be frustrated and lose interest. If the students are practicing a combination, not an exercise, they may improve in performing that particular series of movements, but will not be able to reapply that specific physical knowledge to other tasks.

In answer to my pedagogy student I made the following checklist:

Standing Technique—

> **Feet**: pointing, flex, half toe, isolated joint coordination (ball-toe-ball-flat), foot extensions and brushes off the floor
> **Legs:** swings (loose), gesture (e.g.passee), turned in and out; circles
> **Torso**: straight, round, hollow; swings, contractions (release) curve, arch, wave, spirals, pelvic isolations
> **Arms:** various forms and in coordination with other body parts
> **Focus**: varied, flexible

Whole Body

Plie
Impulses (from various body parts)
Weight transfer
Isolations
Jumps
Placement
Turns
Spirals

Swings
Going to and from the floor

This very general list is meant only as an aid to remembering all the areas that must be covered.

The Floor—its pros and cons

Except for the final moments of "The Dying Swan", a ballerina is hardly ever found on the floor. Modern dance is completely different, as those of us know who have spent time shifting in our seats to get past the head of the person in front of us in order to see what's happening on the stage floor at a modern dance concert.

Aside from the skills needed to go to or rise from the floor (on the above list going to and from the floor), the floor can be a great aid in building certain technical skills.

Strength in the mid-torso is most easily developed on the floor. This area is woefully underdeveloped in today's youngsters who spend most of their time sitting,—in school, in front of the television or the computer, or in the family car, being driven from one place to another. The floor supports the rest of the body as stomach, back or leg muscles are working.

> In the same way, gravity can hold the body as legs move through turned out positions. Once the right hip or shoulder leave the floor when the left leg opens to the side, the body is not properly aligned. The student lying on her back can feel these aberrations easily. It's harder to cheat, and easier to feel what's right.

Stretches for the legs and the lower spine are more efficiently taught on the floor than on the barre. Less can go wrong.

In my early training, classes very often started on the floor. I hated the pain, the lack of movement in space and was always relieved when this part of class was over. If youngsters have a chance to conquer the space, have some fun and raise their cardiovascular rates in improvisational structures beforehand (see "The first ten minutes" in Chapter 2), they are often thankful to sit or lie on the ground, even though their thanks may turn to groans as stomach muscles are worked.

> It is nonproductive and can even be dangerous to stretch cold muscles. For this reason, it is better to do some standing technical exercises after the improvisational structure before going to the floor. Larger, whole-body exercises like body swings, plies and leg gestures can help reestablish the verticality of the body after floor work.

Nobody takes dance classes to do exercises. A limit of 20-25 minutes for technical work in a 60-minute class is maximum. The teacher, seeing all the weaknesses still to be worked on, often tries to do too much. After all, that's what we experienced in professional training: work, sweat, hurt and try again. Most youngsters take one class a week, at the most two. It is easier to kill their joy than it is to build a perfect grand plie. On the long run, there's more to be gained for the students and for the teacher from arousing their curiosity and increasing their understanding, than in technical achievement alone.

Reality Check 4-5 year olds

It's a rainy, cold afternoon. Our teacher has brought a charming picture book to use as a base for work on imagination and improvisation with her first class of the day—four to five years olds who have been dancing for about 2 months. The children run into the studio screaming to each other—"you're 'It'!" "No, I was 'It' last week! You're 'It'". A wild game of Tag is soon in progress. The children are totally involved.

Only 3 students respond to her call to sit in a circle to take attendance. She calls out the others by name, forced to yell over the screams of the running children. After she has finally gotten most of the class seated, the two boys in the class continue to chase each other even more wildly than before. Our teacher stands and tries to catch one of the boys as he runs past, calling "you're 'It'". He slips past her and continues running. Soon four girls have stood up and re-joined the game. Three girls remain seated looking nervously at each other and the teacher. What will she do? What should they do?

The teacher goes to the music and starts the running music. The three girls stand, relieved that a decision has been taken and permission evidently granted to run, and join their classmates. When the teacher pushes the pause button, the whole class freezes, as they have learned to do. She calls out praise for the great shapes she sees, and immediately restarts the music, after calling out "this time run backwards". The children are absorbed in the task at hand are forced to give it their full attention. After the next freeze she asks the class to run as heavily as possible. It gets very loud in the studio. The next phase is, of course, as quietly as possible. When she has stopped the music she gathers the class around her asking if robbers move loudly or softly. She says she will close her eyes and challenges the class to sneak by her so quietly that she does not hear them. When she hears something, she will point in that direction and that person must remain frozen.

What's happening here: In bad weather young children often have a lot of excess energy. As soon as they enter an open and as yet undefined space, they let loose. In the example above, the teacher almost descended to their level in her attempt to stop the boys. Luckily she reached for the music and used it to allow the students to really run off steam.

By slowly adding complications (running backwards) and by seeming to go with the class (as loud as possible) she resumed leadership, finally making it physically clear to the class (move like a robber) that loud and fast are not the only movement choices available, and that if they are continued long enough, can be tiring. The sneaking/robber game involves fooling an adult, always fun for children of this age. They must be very, very careful how they distribute their weight as they creep by. This concentration on weight distribution is tangible, muscular, sensual and involves the imagination of the children, who feel themselves transported into another world.

2

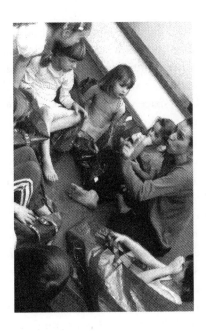

STARTING A NEW CLASS AT VARIOUS AGES

4-6, 6-8, 8-10, 10-12, 12-14, 14-16 years old
Why: *basic premises.* **What**: *the first 10 minutes.* **How**: *teaching tips and
What's Happening Here (analysis)*

The first class:

Imagine you are thrown into a swimming pool. You don't know how deep the
water is or it's temperature. You have to stay afloat and let the water carry you,

not thrash at it wildly. Walking into a new class is a bit like this. The unknown element, the students, can carry you, if you let them.

The very first step is welcoming them and establishing contact in a friendly way. Gathering the class at the beginning—to take attendance, to show a picture or whatever—always gives a sense of commencement and of being together.

It's important to remember that you are in the water with them, not standing on the side, above them and still dry. This means sitting on the floor with them and using your first name, just as they do. Establishing eye contact with each student, learning their names and making sure they know yours (and can say it) is a good way to start.

From here you can move on to non-intimate physical contact, non-threatening spatial associations[1] and then moving through the space. The first moments of movement should be fairly unburdened by stipulations. Older children and young people can handle multi-tasking better than small children for whom simply running alone in a large space with others is a challenge. Any structures used here should be easy to understand and easy to do.

Moving in Space

The single most unusual feature of a dance studio is the empty space. No sofas, coffee tables, rugs and lamps to avoid. It's like a gym, but more neutral. It quite literally leaves you space, it doesn't impose. The exploration of this space can be one of the most liberating and enjoyable elements of a dance class. It also offers a unique opportunity to experience responsibility and communality firsthand. The young dancers must make split second decisions about where they are in space, where they want to go, and what that will entail. For very young children this alone is a challenge. For older children who have been trained or schooled in a more authoritarian and tightly structured environment, the problem of avoiding a collision with another dancer can be next to insoluble. At a demonstration class, working with children from 8 to 14 years old whose background was only in classical ballet, I was amazed to see even the older students using their arms as snowplows to push others out of the way. For these, as for most children whatever their age or background, these problems diminished with each repetition.

These opening moments are give and take, the teacher can observe, and so can the students—how does she react to humor, to proximity, to touching, what are

---

1.   For some children any physical contact can be threatening, even holding hands. Simply sitting beside strangers is a challenge. Shared activities, like clapping, saying names, helps to gradually diminish fear of contact.

her body clothes—the physical postures and movements that have been adapted over time to show the outside world "who I am". They're particularly valuable, as no forms have been introduced. We're not "dancing"; we're just all here together in the water with a minimum of rules to avoid chaos. When the chaos does occur—collisions, confusions—it's a good moment to gather the class and introduce, seriously and with great emphasis, the **ground rules:**

> **you cannot purposely hurt another person or endanger her**
> **you cannot laugh at anyone**

In contrast, game rules like "use the whole space", "each one has her own path" can be delivered while the class is moving.

This opening phase, which can be the first 10 minutes of a 60 or 90 minute class, remains the initial point of contact no matter what age the students are or how long they have been dancing. It is the moment when they really enter the class, leaving the baggage of school, friends and family behind, and giving you the opportunity to remind yourself of them, individually and as a group. (In a typical teaching day, handling 3-5 different age levels and groups, this orientation can be very useful).

The first 10 minutes

Here are some suggestions for the first 10 minutes for different ages. Each suggestion is followed by "what's happening here?" an analysis of the processes, which can help the teacher to develop her own structures, and by "teaching points",—what to emphasize, what to avoid during the structure.

4-6 yrs., new group:

Names, clapping: sitting in a circle on the floor, after each has said her name, the class repeats it, clapping the rhythm that the syllables of the name make: le-a-NO-re.

Moving: run with music, stop on silence. When the music starts again, running in a different direction (front, side, backwards). Frozen figures can be added in the stop phase (a monster is an easy start, later calling it a shape is just as suggestive, and acquaints the students with a dance term).

What's happening here?

This exchange of information is important and establishes community. The rhythm of the names is a step toward dance without being threatening. It's a novel approach to something each one knows very well,—her own name. A group is constructed through the sharing of names, the fact that all clap together. During the running each dancer decides where she will go and how to avoid collisions. She takes responsibility for herself. The stops in the music are audio training, but they're also a non-threatening challenge (Can you hear it? What do you do?). The monster allows the dancers to try out, without thinking "pretty" "graceful" or "dancing"

Teaching Points:

> The rhythmic qualities in the name are picked up by the teacher who leads the class clapping the rhythm immediately after each dancer says her name.
>
> The teacher should not run from the beginning with the class, rather describing beforehand, verbally and with hand gestures, all the different possible paths, as well as the impossible ones (out of the studio, under the piano).
>
> Review possible monster shapes before the game starts, asking the students to show, all at once, not individually, how a monster could look. At this point, the teacher can already refer to the "monsters" as "shapes", acquainting the students with the proper term.
>
> The class should be praised for complete stops, and stillness. Corrections should be general, directed to the entire class: "Are your eyes moving?" "Are you really frozen? What about your toes?".
>
> Guidance for the running can be called out above the music "Each one leaves her own trail in the snow/on the sand".
>
> Music should be clear, rhythmic and pleasant, upbeat.

6-8 yrs. New group: names clapping with hands, feet, bottoms.
Moving: 1) running to music, freeze on silence or move to instruments in each non-music phase; 2) stepping to drum

What's happening here?

Clapping the name rhythm as with the 4-6 year olds, but with hands, feet and bottoms upsets preconceptions about what dance class is. It's silly, making them laugh, and forces them to use their bodies in new ways. Moving to the instruments stimulates—what my ears hear, my body does-, taking the dancers into new motor patterns and dynamics through the imagination. Drumming for the class gives a sense of responsibility. Moving to the drum is audio training.

Teaching points:

Moving to instruments: The choice of instruments is important. Drums and cymbals are ubiquitous and always useful. A trip to a good music store can reveal treasures that are sometimes inexpensive, Chinese bowl gongs, whistles, cachichis, etc. The visual attraction of the instruments is important. If possible, avoid the "rice in a can" alternative. You may find it imaginative and certainly less expensive, but for a child it remains exactly that,—rice in a can. At the very least, paint the can in attractive colors.

The drummer should be a volunteer, after the teacher has done several clear repetitive rhythms. The rhythms should suggest movement (gallop, run-run-jump) dynamics or size (loud and slow for big steps; light and fast for small steps etc.).

The teacher dances as she drums, indicating the possible variations in size and dynamics. She can dance with the class when a student drums. The phases should be short, so that no one dancer becomes "leader" for too long. The teacher should make sure that the drum is passed on at the proper time.

8-10 yrs. New group: each one says her name. Running to music with changing directions: backwards, sideways, on one foot, on 2 feet and one hand, with your feet off the ground, only on your bottom, etc.

What's happening here?

This age group, with its enormous motoric vigor and energy, enjoys the puzzle of finding out how to run with 2 feet and one hand, or with no foot on the ground.

Teaching points:

> The music should be rhythmically clear and energetic.
> Emphasize the use of the entire space.
> Give corrections when you see inaccuracies, but without naming names. This reminds the students that there is a right and wrong way to do even volitional movements,—a vital lesson for more structured exercises.

10-12 yrs. New group: names, running to music, running in 2s, in 3s, in 4,s in 6s alternating with running alone and in different directions. The teacher calls out the changes over the music.

What's happening here?

The task of running is non-threatening, but having to find one or several partners while doing it can be a challenge. It all goes by so fast that no time is left for joining your best friend. The constantly changing task brings group feeling alternating with individual responsibility. For the teacher, this structure offers an insight into group dynamics: is there one leader of the group of 5 or 6? Who follows? Does anyone split off? Who gets drawn into a group first, who, last? The non-binding, ever-changing configurations allow the dancers proximity, usually welcome at this age level, without intimacy, which can be threatening.

Teaching points:

> Make sure the class does not run in a circle, something they're accustomed to from gym class.
> The groups, once formed, must stay together until a different direction is given.

12-14 yrs. new group; Names. Running to music stopping on silence, then following directions for actions (shake and freeze different body parts, swing, throw the movement somewhere like a ball, throw the movement 2 directions—there and there; draw an imaginary continuous line with a body part (e.g. your elbow) around yourself while standing still, leaving no space empty (behind you, between legs, around feet), continuing the line without breaking off; change body parts at will, e.g. drawing with the head, earlobe or knee. Erase the drawing with both hands—all of it. Drawing and erasing should be one action phase). Alternate running to music with each action phase. The music should be rhythmically clear and upbeat, positive, not in a minor key.

What's happening here?

The constantly changing spatial configurations (who is near you on the stop, who can you see, who not) provide variety. The simple directions provide no technical challenges, at the same time being different from daily movement. Everyone does it a little differently,—it's impossible to shake your arm exactly like your best friend—a relief from peer pressure, so strong in this age group. Each student is part of the whole, which feels good, and doing the same thing, but a bit differently.

14-16 yrs. new group: Names. Special Circle: The class stands in a large circle. The teacher explains that the whole group will walk along the periphery.
The teacher starts by standing in the middle of the circle and calling out and doing a task. The tasks should be easy at first and situated in the middle of the circle of walking dancers,—e.g. lying on your back and counting out loud or hopping up and down and clapping.
The teacher initiates every action, describing it verbally as she does it. When the teacher stops and returns to the circle, some other dancer must take over immediately. Once an action has been introduced, someone must continue it. This is the group's responsibility.
Whoever takes over the task does it as long as she wants to and follows the rules, returning to the circle when she is tired of doing the task.
After the teacher leaves the center of the circle and a dancer has taken over the first action, the teacher initiates a new action.
The actions accumulate until 5-10 dancers (depending on the size of the class) are involved in individual actions as the rest of the class walks the circle's periphery.

> Example: The center of the circle is filled with a whistling, clapping dancer, one who gets up and lies down continually, one dancer singing "Yankee Doodle", one dancer swinging her legs back and forth, one dancer saying no continually.

Eventually some actions can be assigned taking place outside the circle (run along with your hand on the barre, calling out your name; or hop back and forth between the window and the door, etc.) and some needing more than one person (one person tries to do a handstand on the wall and another helps).

The tasks should be fairly easy to do, pointless and noticeable. By the time you've got 8 tasks going the class is thoroughly shaken up, watching all directions, functioning as a group—and usually laughing!

What's happening here?

This exercise, which I first did with Bill T. Jones and Arnie Zane, is fun and surprising. It forms a sense of community, forcing all students into an active role. The concentration needed to watch all the tasks in and outside the circle widens the focus from the frontal, usual in school, to a much broader consciousness of what is going on in the entire space. At the end of the exercise there is a real sense of having gotten rid of the baggage that young people of this age carry with them,—problems in school, at home, with boy- or girlfriends. The class is ready to face new work with an open mind.

Teaching points:

Emphasize that the changeover is initiated by the performer giving up, not by someone bumping her out of her activity. This distributes responsibility and prevents more confident students from dominating.
The group should be at least 12 dancers. The larger the group, the more tasks can be assigned, the more focus is broadened.
The teacher participates, walking around the circle with the class and initiating each new task.

She reminds the group of actions which must be performed ("no-one is whistling and laying on her back").
The tasks should be possible for anyone to do, not dance-related.
Change the direction of the walking after a certain time, to prevent dizziness.

After all of these games

>The cardiovascular rate should be raised,
>the student should have a vague idea of her fellow students,—what they look like, what they're called.
>The student follows rules, which still allow some freedom of choice.
>A community is established.
>The teacher offers options, but does not dictate.

.... Here we are all dancing together. But is this dancing? is the question that comes from many parents and some children. These structures allow the students to become aware of their own bodies, of the space and of their fellow students. They facilitate the teaching goals listed in 'Basic Principles'.

Reality Check: 6-7 year olds

It's an afternoon in mid-October. Our teacher has brought chestnuts and autumn leaves and some beautiful music with her, which she hopes will stimulate her class of 6-7 year olds to an improvisation on autumn. There are four new-comers in the class, 6 year olds who are in their first year of school. The other 5 children are in their second year at school and have been taking dance classes for 2 years.

As she enters the studio the children stop their games of tag and surround our teacher—all except Suzanne and Pauline, 2 of the old-timers from last year, who stop playing and survey the situation from the barre across the room. The class settles on the floor in a circle around the teacher for the usual ritual of taking attendance. Pauline and Suzanne remain where they are and call out "not here" when their names are called from the list.

As the teacher shows the autumn leaves the children crowd around, all except Suzanne und Pauline who demonstratively sit on the floor and talk to each other. It's noticeable that Suzanne is the leader. She sits on the floor first and pulls Pauline, who otherwise might become interested in the leaves, down with her. All this is noticed by our teacher who has decided to ignore their behavior.

After the children contribute their observations about autumn leaves, the teacher puts on the music and invites the class to blow around like the autumn leaves in the wind. As the children start to run Suzanne slides to the middle of the floor, Pauline slithers right after her. They make themselves as wide and bother-some as possible. The class runs around them absorbed in being autumn leaves.

The teacher stops the music, gathers the class in the center of the studio and compliments the class on their 'leafiness'. She asks them if they have noticed that leaves sometimes get stuck onto or inside objects, like trees or shopping carts that stand outside supermarkets or on the seats of swings at playgrounds. She points to Pauline and Suzanne, still prone on the floor of the studio, and says that they are some sort of objects, could there be 2 more. She chooses 2 volunteers and asks them what sort of objects they are and how they are shaped. These volunteers assume the shape of the objects. The game starts again, this time with 4 immobile dancers in the room, 2 of them in shapes. The leaves become stuck on the objects, filling in the empty spaces in their shapes, even in Suzanne's and Pauline's shapes. The teacher quickly announces that 4 other dancers can be shapes and that this time, when a leaf gets stuck, the object becomes a leaf (mobile) and the leaf becomes the object (immobile). Suzanne and Pauline remain where they are, but, as this cycle commences, leaves stick to them and they are liberated to join the game.

What's happening here?

The two veterans are determined to show their superiority. Already in the second grade and experienced in dance class too, they are not as easily entranced as the newcomers. Their response to the attendance list ('not here') is meant to call the teacher's attention and to single themselves out of the crowd. Their non-participation in the game is provocative, (children could fall over them) and counter-productive, (others could be attracted to the revolution). The teacher's initial lack of attention only stimulates the two to more aggressive action (lying on the floor).

It's important to remember, if possible, that actions like these have very little relation to what the teacher is offering. She could show the most fascinating object, play the most beautiful music, initiate totally new structures, it would make no difference. Calling attention to the two by calling their names, or urging them to join, would only encourage them and could easily escalate into a contest between our teacher and the two challengers. By incorporating their immobility into the game, the teacher offers them a way out of their isolation without the humiliation of having to give up their positions. They have become integrated without coercion.

3

INTRODUCING IMPROVISATION

Why: Most people are afraid of improvisation—as a concept and as an activity. Although almost everyone moves instinctively to music, the idea of doing it "on command" is inhibiting. This goes for dance teachers, dancers and normal humans, in fact even more for dancers and dance teachers. Professional dance education emphasizes achievement, attaining skills,—"doing it right".

On the other hand, everyone is more present in the movement when they're doing their own movement, be it in a club, in the living room or in the studio. A bit like singing in the shower, it seems to need privacy or, at least, a sense of being "alone with yourself". That sense of involvement is one of the things that make improvisation so fascinating to watch and so rewarding to do. It is one of the richest sources of renewal in dance and, for children to a certain extent, and especially for teenagers, one of the hardest things to attain.

It is vital to begin with improvisational structures from the very first class. Improvisation is not something that can be introduced "when the class is far enough along", nor can it be inserted to liven up a dull class or wake up passive students. It must be there from the beginning of the course and should be present in some form in every lesson.

How:

The first contact with improvisation is simple to arrange. All the structures in "the First 10 minutes" section of the second chapter, with the exception of Special Circle, use improvisation. There are no forms given for making a monster, no rhythms given for drumming.

These structures make improvisation easy because the directions are clear, the parameters easy to recognize and, because everyone is moving at once, the situation is non-threatening. Basically everyone is doing individual improvisations simultaneously.

From the above statements we can make a list of positive guidelines:

1. **Make directions clear**
2. **Establish clear parameters**
3. **Create a supportive, non-threatening atmosphere**

Using these guidelines, let's move on to more complicated structures whose main aim is movement exploration.[1]

What

The Rational Approach: "if you name it—you own it"

Very often students are puzzled when asked what kinds of movements we do when we dance. Defining generic terms makes dance more tangible to students. (Incidentally, this can help students to answer questions from parents or friends about what they really do in dance class.) Once identified, movement becomes familiar, a tool, in Marion Gough's words: "if you name it—you own it".[2]

---

1. For other uses of improvisation see Chapter 6 on Group Improvisation for methods of integrating a group, heightening awareness; and Chapter 5 for developing skills.
2. Dance educator. Former Senior Lecturer in Dance, Laban Centre, London

One way to initiate this is to ask the class to show, simultaneously, a fall, a turn or a jump. Students 8 years and older understand gesture (a movement without transfer of weight). All students understand locomotive movement. (Remember this is not a chance to work on a dance dictionary. Just general terms are needed at this point.) Praise the different forms these movements can take, encouraging the students' choices, increasing their self-confidence and emphasizing the multiple possibilities. It helps to write these terms on a board or flip chart, so the students can refer to them as they work.

Here some examples of clear directions:

a) 8-10 yrs., 10-12 yrs.

move from one corner to the other using a jump, a turn and a fall plus anything else necessary to get from one corner to the other.

b) 4-6 yrs., 6-8 yrs:

standing in place draw a pattern/design in the air with one body part, then with another

c) 8-10 yrs.:

move through a jungle full of hanging vines, sharp stones, bushes and broad streams holding your hands as if they were tied behind your back.

d)10-12 yrs.,12-14 yrs.:

think of three generic movements (e.g. turn, jump, fall, walk, skip, run. leap, etc.). Find an order you like and can remember. Do the movements one after another making the connections smooth. Now think of a place and shape for the beginning and for the end.

e) 10-12 yrs., 12-14 yrs.:

think of five generic movements you know, write them on a piece of paper (turn, jump, fall, walk, skip, run, leap) and do them in a specific time (8 counts, or a music phrase) or spatial path (in a circle, from one corner to the other, crossing the stage). The paper can serve as a reference for the observers: has the dancer included everything? is the order as planned?

In the examples above, the parameters are clear: go from here to there, use this much time, move these body parts because of this situation.

The Imaginative Approach

This introductory phase can be completely different,—more sensual, more imaginative,—through the presentation of objects. A flowing silk scarf, a high-bouncing ball, a feather, even a pencil or an eraser move in different ways, incorporate different dynamics. The challenge of moving like one of these objects, or any other, can present a huge leap of faith for the students. First they have to see or picture the movement of the object, then transfer that movement to their body. This is easier for smaller children, but very difficult for 12 or 13 year olds. By limiting the parameters—can you move your hand like an eraser, your leg like a pencil, your spine like the silk scarf—you present a less threatening bridge into the suspension of disbelief, a vital step toward improvisation.

Teaching tips:

>The more detailed the directions, the easier it is for students to engage in the improvisation. It's easier to move an arm than to move your whole body like a pencil.

>Describing the situation in the jungle precisely,—hanging vines, broad streams, sharp stones,—helps to physically envision the jungle, and incidentally involves different body parts—arms, torso and feet.

>The direction "with your hands behind your back" prevents pantomimic actions and brings the torso more into play as an instrument of expression.

Any object presented should be pregnant with movement possibilities, at least in the teacher's mind. It's important to take this step in the preparation of the class, not simply to present the object, no matter how fascinating it may seem at first sight. Even a piece of paper can stimulate movement—torn, flat and pristine, shredded, crushed into a ball, burning. An eraser shrinks, becomes shreds, a raindrop rolls down a window, is blown by the wind, dries up, joins a puddle (ah, group improv!).[3] To prevent a pantomimic reaction it helps to segment the movement. The moment the staple leaves the stapler, for example, rather than how a stapler moves, which is fairly limited.

By asking the students the right questions beforehand, the teacher stimulates imagination and still leaves choices open.

>Is the stapler hard or soft?
>Can it move in many different ways or only a few?

---

3.   These examples illustrate a vital point,—the difference between dance and pantomime. Pantomime is meant to represent a place, situation or object that we can recognize, that is familiar to us. In the example of the jungle, the recognition of where the vines are hanging, the temperature and speed of the water in the stream are important for pantomime. For the dance improvisation it is the qualities of the movement, not their precision and storytelling qualities that are important.

>What could happen to a stapler?
>How would that effect the movement?

Like signposts in a forest, these questions should indicate a general direction, without prescribing the exact path.

Young dance students always ask if they have to remember the improvisation. We know how difficult this can be. If the directions and the parameters are clear, it's easier to remember the improvisations, if not movement for movement, at least in general, which is enough.

A description of what you envision, what you'd like to see, and the movements you think suitable will not be helpful to students. It's very important to keep your own compositional ambitions in the non-improvisational part of the class. Commenting on an improvisation by saying, "That doesn't please me" or "That isn't what I wanted" is counterproductive on many levels.

>It is dishonest, seemingly giving the students freedom to do what they want, and then withdrawing it.
>It takes responsibility from the students, making the teacher the sole authority.
>It puts prime emphasis on pleasing the teacher rather than exploring possibilities, and incidentally
>reveals the inadequacy of the directions.

Even in a compositional situation, when improvisation is being used to find movement patterns for a dance, the parameters should remain descriptive, the evaluation impersonal. Then the students can judge for themselves if the aims and the parameters are met, taking part actively in the dance-making process.

As a general rule, it's always helpful during class preparation to think, "What could go wrong here?" In working on technique or on a combination, the teacher knows the pitfalls and the aims, the wrongs and the rights. Using improvisation, she must sort out her aims and her means ahead of time. In this way, some pitfalls may be avoided, and the process is clearer to her and, hopefully, to the class.

Even after a thorough preparation and giving very clear directions, an improvisation can "miss the mark". It helps to find something positive, something you or the students find interesting. Ask them why it's interesting for them. Could it be a pause? a change of dynamics? of direction? Having found what it is for the students (and it may not be the element you have identified) they can try again, using this or any other changes. Trying to pin down the problem can help to find its solution, but it's also important to look for what's right, no matter how small a detail it is. Eliciting their help in the detective work engages their active participation as viewers. Young dance students who have participated in this sort of class will never be at a loss later to explain why they liked a dance (or didn't).

Watching and evaluating

In contrast to the structures outlined in the chapter on the first ten minutes, improvisations later in the class should be shown and evaluated. This is the time to develop the non-threatening atmosphere.

>Students can show the improvisation in small groups, without the exposure of dancing alone so that the teacher can see what's happening.
>The observers should be reminded of the parameters before watching the work.

>After seeing the improvisations, the observers comment on what they have seen, using the parameters as standards and remaining impersonal in their comments ("I saw ..." rather than "Jane didn't ...").

By making general, non-personal comments, referring only to the directions and parameters given, the teacher and the observers maintain a non-threatening atmosphere. The teacher can provide guidance without being censorious. The students are protected.

For solo improvisations, the dancers can perform three at a time.

>It helps to assign "watchers" for each dancer, so that the audience does not float off into passivity. The observers can also be asked to make sure each of the directions is fulfilled. Jane watches to see if there are 3 different movements, Anne observes the changes in direction and Pauline watches the body parts involved. Giving out these watching assignments, incidentally, reminds the dancers of the directions.

The process of observing should be as active for the students watching as it is for the performers, but it can only be so if the discussion is precisely guided. This helps to take the mystery out of improvisation, and with it the fear of not being "creative" enough. The students are just finding their own paths through the forest, from signpost, to signpost. The clearer the directions, the easier they are to follow, the less threatening improvisation can be.

Improvisation in itself breaks up the traditional structure of the class: the teacher as giver of information, the students as recipients. In this way it empowers, encourages independence and inspires self-confidence.

Music and Improvisation

Paradoxically, music can serve as a powerful stimulant or as an inhibitor to movement. When the music becomes too dominant, it forces the dancer onto one particular path through the forest, instead of letting the body's own movement lead. This independence, the ability to listen to the body not to the music, is not something that comes naturally, certainly not to children and young people.

Music can bridge initial inhibitions, like a friend dancing with you. Teenagers spend much of their lives plugged in to music on walkmen, mp3 players etc. They are used to constant music. Younger children often cannot maintain the initial exuberance that leads to movement or lack the concentration to maintain an inner narrative, which might carry them. Music can help.

Music can also be the source and purpose of an improvisational structure. Being able to hear the mood, rhythmic changes, the structure of music will help stimulate movement. A very intense piece with a strongly defined mood can help set the tone of the improvisation and maintain the mood through interruptions and distractions. On the other hand, when the music is too complex,—with large orchestrations, for example, or extremely complicated rhythmic structures or changes, the urge to move can be throttled, not stimulated.

Certain kinds of music or sounds lay down an acoustic background, dissolving the silence which is often threatening for young people, without imposing a specific mood or motor impulse. These sounds help maintain concentration, filling the void which otherwise would probably be filled with children commenting, directing each other, or just chatting.

Popular music,—pop, rock, and rap etc.—produces "popular" movement: what the youngsters see on MTV, which leaves little room for creativity or personal expression. Although it can be used in other parts of class where a solid beat is required, it is not productive for improvisation. Boom-boom music most often produces boom-boom dancing.

Musical taste is extremely personal. Topping any list of music, which should not be used in class—any part of class-, is music that the teacher does not like. Once that has been eliminated, the choices become more difficult. Unfortunately, nothing can eliminate the hours spent in a music store, or listening to the radio in the car and at home, or going to concerts and the theater. Ultimately, the choice of this very important element is up to the individual.

Often students, who also have personal taste in music, will ask the teacher to use certain music. If it's possible for the teacher to use the music in class, it is very positive for the class environment. However, if the teacher can't bear the music, if it throttles more than motivates, I see nothing wrong in explaining that the music may perhaps be wonderful in other places, but doesn't work in a dance class.

Where to look in music stores:

Music stores are confusing places. Here are some of the categories I examine first, and music I have found there:

Film/show Scores: "Lola Runs", "Cape Fear", "Crossing the Bridge"; Rene Aubrey, Cirque du Soleil

percussionists including Dudu Tucci, Albrecht Riermeier, Les Tambours du Bronx, Kodo and Steve Reich

electronic including Philip Glass (especially the film score from "Anima Mundi"), John Cage, Steve Reich

world/ethnic: Radio Tarifa, Rabih Abou-Khalil, Gypsy Kings, Kronos playing music from Africa

classical music: Benjamin Britten, Dvorjak "New World Symphony", Debussy, Poulenc, Milhaud, Honegger, Copeland

instrumentalists: whichever instruments suit the occasion

rock (for 15-18 yr olds) Radiohead, Einsturzende Neubauten

Reality Check 8-10 year olds

Eva runs into the studio. After hanging on the barre from all parts of her eight-year-old body she runs to our teacher who is looking for her CDs. Joined by Louisa and Isabel who have been playing "Tag", she asks the teacher "What will we do today?" "A surprise" "What kind of surprise?" "Can we use the scarves? the gymnastic balls?" Oh Yes! gym balls! gym balls! gym balls!" 12 healthy 8-10 year olds scream in that horrible singsong, left over from pre-school days. Perhaps our teacher answers instead "you'll find out soon enough". Immediately comes the chant "gym balls! gym balls! gym balls!" Or she says, "Today we will do something really nice". Guess what she hears? Right: "gym balls! gym balls! gym balls!" Or she says, "Today we're going to dance". The answers: "but no mats" "but no technique" "only jumping" "gym balls!" and then everybody screams "gym balls! gym balls! gym balls!"

Our teacher can say "I've planned something else, but we can do 5 minutes with the balls at the end of class". But she really has to do it otherwise she loses credibility. Or she can say "I've planned something else, but we can work with the balls next week. I'll write it in my book so that I don't forget. Now let's start." Again, she has to really write it and, although it may be forgotten by the time the next class rolls around, it is important to keep her promise, using the balls for technique or for an improv.

What's happening here?

These dancers are testing their teacher. Unsure of what the possibilities are, they pick out their current favorite activity. Who is going to decide what happens in the class?

Our teacher wants to maintain control, but also to show the students respect. Under the motto if you want to get respect, you have to give it—she treats the students' wishes as she would like her wishes to be treated by them. Having allowed space for their wishes, she proceeds with her plans.

4

INTRODUCING COMPOSITIONAL FORMS

Composing means imposing a form on something not consciously structured. It is a tool. Teaching youngsters composition is as necessary as teaching them technique. It gives them a sense of mastery, of ownership, enlarging their movement vocabulary and deepening their understanding of movement.

A combination, using the elements already mastered and adding new ones, for the purpose of mastering them, is purpose-driven. As such, it is assembled but not composed. It is not the same as choreography and should not be called that.

One can compose a dance as a whole or its sections or the movement per se using various methods and formulae. Those of us who have gone through a course in composition know how dry this can be. Used properly however, compositional tools can provide variety, clarity, depth and direction to a dance.

Rather than starting with a flip chart list and a lecture, let's play a game (and all ages enjoy this, the younger ones who still like to play, the older ones for the surprise element and the equity of the process).

Before class, write down each direction printed below on separate pieces of paper.

> **Is it possible to do it as slowly as possible?**
> **Is it possible to do it as fast as possible?**
> **Is it possible to do with stops and starts?**
> **Is it possible to do making a milkshake—mixing up slow, fast, stops and starts?**

Then in class let each student make a simple movement chain that includes, for example, a locomotive movement, a turn, a jump and a fall. After she has completed her movement chain let each student draw a paper from a container (hat, drum, bowl) and rework her chain according to the question on the paper. Now let three dancers at a time show first their original chains, then the changes from the papers. Ask the class:

> How does each version feel for the dancer?
> How different do the versions look to the observers?
> Which was more interesting—with or without the changes?
> Can you identify which change (piece of paper) each dancer chose?

Then let the groups of three choose a paper with one possibility out of the following:

What happens when 3 dancers do their individual chains

> **close together?**
> **far apart?**
> **with one facing away from the observers and 2 facing them?**
> **all three in a far away corner of the space?**
> **all three across the front of the space?**

For dancers from 8 yrs. on:

> **What if one dancer performs her movement chain only with her hands?**
> **another, only with her pelvis, a third, only with her head?**

Ask the class:

> >How did these changes affect the dancers? the viewers?
> >Which was the most interesting?
> >Was one was hard to watch? Why?

Then let the groups choose one each from the following:

> **What happens if 6 people learn one movement chain and perform it simultaneously?**
> **How does the chain look if the turn and fall are repeated 10 times before completing the chain as planned?**
> **Dance the movement chain in a hurricane and then in a foggy forest.**

Questions for the class:

> >Which did you like better as a dancer?
> >As a viewer?
> >Why,—more interesting? more differences?
> >What made it more interesting or more varied?

If the words contrast, different time, different space, dynamics, different relationships between the dancers come up, write them on the flip chart/board. These are compositional elements which must be considered when making a dance. Instrumentation,—which body part or how many dancers perform the movement—will probably be a new concept for the class. It is a very valuable compositional tool.

This, of course, is not a recommendation for one class, but rather a list of possibilities which can be experimented with off and on throughout the school year. Composition comes into its own during the preparation of any performance. Referring back to these experiments, the teacher can give group assignments for varying the basic movement that has already been developed, either by her or by the students. The class feels it has influenced the finished product and helped make it happen. (See Chapter 8 "Making a Dance") It becomes more than ever their dance, not something that has been imposed on them.

Tools

One can compose a dance as a whole or its sections using the following forms:

>beginning—middle—end;
>canon, the same movement phrase repeated at successive intervals
>fugue, one or two themes repeated or imitated by successively entering figures and developed contrapuntally in a continuous interweaving of the movements.
>theme & variations, All variations are related to the theme movement
> rondo, one theme repeated between unrelated movement phrases:
ABACADAEAFAG...
>ABA,
>AB;

or work on the movement per se using

>time—slow motion, speedup and all variations between, fractured and mixed, stops,
> space—body to stage (where the dancer is on the stage),
body to body (where the dancers are in relationship to each other),
body within itself (size of movement)
>instrumentation—body parts used, numbers of dancers used
>retrograde and repetition. Retrograde is performing the movement exactly as it appears on the rewind of a video machine. It is very difficult to puzzle out. Advanced dancers often gain insights to new movements during the process. Observers seldom recognize retrograde unless the original and the retrograde are performed successively repeatedly. There is a certain familiarity—where have I seen this before. It is, like all the other tools, simply another way of manipulating the movement.
>dynamic/effort
>forms of canon, fugue, theme & variations, ABA, AB etc. dealing only with sections of movement

All of these manipulations are simply that,—manipulations that vary the dance, perhaps shifting emphasis or meaning. Like being able to go to or rise from the floor, to jump, to turn, to orient oneself in space, to dance with or against the music, they can provide huge variety for the performer. For the viewer they provide the comfort of familiarity through repetition and pattern.

Reality Check: 13 year olds

It's a rainy spring day. Our teacher has just finished an energetic class with her 8 to 10 year olds. She opens the windows and goes to the music to sort out her notes and music for the next class.

Slowly one 13 year old enters. Her gaze on the floor, she greets the teacher inaudibly and walks slowly along the edge of the studio to the far corner, away from the door, the teacher, the music and the 2 girls who enter talking quietly and intensely to each other. The rest of the class enters in twos and threes. They glance over to the teacher, then settle, ignoring her, some sitting on the floor, some standing, and continue their conversations. The last girl stands in the doorway, neither in nor out, looking first at the groups in the studio, then into the dressing room. The last student joins her finally.

The teacher summons the class together. Those on the floor slide over without getting up; the others walk over and settle down on the floor. The teacher greets the class, takes attendance. Her question "how are you" is answered with groans. Some flop backward so that they're lying prone on the floor.

The teacher's plan: really shaking this class up, getting them to concentrate on technique, and finally cleaning up the combination for the annual performance. The problems: Low energy, exhaustion, real or imagined, lack of curiosity; cliques and friendships that still dominate the group. One outsider.

Abandoning her plans, she goes to the music, quickly takes out the Turkish rap music she had prepared for running, replacing it with Al-Jadida, by Rabih Abou-Khalil, track 2, but doesn't start it yet. She tells the students to find a place on the floor that's at least 3 meters away from anyone else or the walls, to lie on their backs, close their eyes and feel what body parts have contact with the floor. She tells the class to slowly press all the parts of their body into the floor, one after the other, not forgetting nape of the neck, armpits, the insides of the legs, etc. When she sees that all parts have had contact with the floor, she starts the music, very low volume, asking them to imagine that they're on a soft rug and should try to roll slowly, bringing as many body parts as possible into contact with the floor. As she increases the music volume, she tells them to increase tempo and intensity of the rolls, never staying still in one position, making it easy for themselves, trying out different levels, moving through sitting, kneeling and even coming to standing, never stopping movement, letting rolling movement carry them around the space, bouncing off the walls, always returning to the floor in between. In addition when they come close to someone they can give each other "a high five" or gently tap that person. Close to the end of the 9:33 minutes of music, she tells the dancers to find their way to standing and remain there.

The class continues with stretches and torso roll downs (track 3 of the same CD) remaining in the scattered positions for these, as well as for further technical exercises.

What's happening here?

By starting lying on the floor the students can relax. The continuous music and ever-changing instructions do not leave the students time to develop resistance. The teenage tendency to physical exhaustion is catered to here, not countered, eventually leading to intense physical activity and random contact with "others" in the class, breaking up the cliques, moving the body in unfamiliar ways through unfamiliar paths.

Having achieved tabula rasa, our teacher can either return to her class plan, or continue the unusual by concentrating on rehearsing the combination without working on technique, this time giving corrections that have not been mentioned before.

It's important not to use this structure too often.

5

INCREASING SKILLS

In the normal world of children's dance, students have an hour a week to dance, minus vacations, friends' birthday parties, various children's' illnesses and the times when whoever is providing transport is unable to do so. From the ages of 4 to about 9 years it is almost enough within this narrow time frame to offer challenges suitable to the developmental changes in the students.

From the age of 10 on, young dance students enjoy progress and they want to experience it. They are more critical of the teacher, themselves and what they do. In addition, they are more capable of abstraction. This is the time to present clear technical problems as such and provide possible solutions. Optimally these solutions should produce some tangible improvement within the class time. If this approach is successful, the reason for technical work becomes clear to the students.

Let's take as an example the problem of placement and balance.

Placement is usually referred to as the positioning of the torso, arms and legs in such a way as to facilitate and not hinder movement. This positioning pertains mainly to classical dance. It is based on aesthetic values of the 1700s and on the physical requirements meant to allow the performance of set movements, which satisfy these values, on point and off. It's important to remember that postures and positions we learned in early training are usually based on these values.

The aim of placement in modern dance is to prevent injury and allow maximum mobility. Pushing a student's posterior into place and inflating the ribcage to pull in the stomach will not facilitate mobility.

One way of working in this area is to raise consciousness not only of movement possibility but also of control. Once a student has explored stretching and bending the spine, the movement possibilities of the pelvis, the effect of movement in the shoulder girdle on other body parts, it becomes more possible for her to control these areas and to "place" them where they can be of most benefit to the movement and can best prevent injury. As necessary as doing the exercises themselves is talking about them with the students. The reflection phase doesn't need to be long, but it does need to be precise. Sometimes it is enough to attempt the opposite and let the students draw their own conclusions.

Exercises for balance, torso

1. Lying on back on floor, arms extended to the side, knees bent, soles of feet on floor, hips, knees and feet in one line, roll up and down the spine leaving head on floor, starting with the pelvis on the way up and with the neck on the way down. Be careful to articulate each vertebra individually.

Talking points: How many vertebrae could you count on the way up? on the way down? What muscles do you have to use to go up and down slowly? Is it possible to move your spine this way when you're standing on your feet? Is it harder or easier on the floor? Why?

2. Lying on back on floor, legs extended, arms extended to the sides, lift sternum as if it were being pulled to ceiling, leaving shoulders, head, arms passive. When the sitting position is reached, relax over legs with rounded spine then roll back down to original position vertebrae by vertebrae starting with pelvis. (chest lift)

Talking Points: What's the most active part of your body? the most inactive?

3. Standing: lift shoulders up and down 8 times, them forward and back 8 times. Circle shoulders forward 8 times, then backwards 8 times. Then circle one shoulder forward as the other one is circling backward, reverse

Talking Points: What body parts tend to move with the shoulders? Can you move just your shoulders, leaving all other body parts still?

4. Sitting on floor legs crossed, hands relaxed in lap, slump down so that sternum and navel are closer, then stretch spine so that crown of head is as close as possible to ceiling. Look up to ceiling without changing spine, then lift sternum so that upper back and shoulder girdle are open to ceiling without lifting shoulders. Return to center (crown of head to ceiling). Relax over, head to feet and repeat.

Talking Points: What does your torso feel like when the crown of the head is closest to the ceiling? Can you feel a stretch in the muscles at the end of the exercise (head to feet)? which ones? when you look up at the ceiling? which ones?

Once the students are aware of the necessary work, they should be allowed the chance to use their spine, torso, shoulders in a combination or improvisation that focuses mainly on these areas.

Other technical areas, which always require work, are:

Area	Learning Goal
coordination	control
feet	strength, mobility
legs	strength, mobility/flexibility, control
arms	consciousness, control
focus	consciousness, control

It's helpful to maintain a written record for yourself including the talking points. That way, you can refer back to previous work when the problem arises again in a different sequence. If you're very lucky, the students will remember the work and apply it. At the very least it gives them a sense of continuity and recognition.

Other possibilities:

>performing foot exercises on a count of seven (7/4) or five (5/4) instead of the usual four or eight (2/4, 4/4 meter)

>adding to a familiar exercise by using a different front for each repetition

>inserting balances in leg exercises

>adding contrasting arms or torso contractions to foot or leg work

>changing the eye focus

Shock and awe is perhaps not the best method for presenting challenges, often causing only frustration and hopelessness. But sometimes a little shock is healthy, presenting new fields to conquer. This is especially true if only one element in an exercise is truly difficult and the rest is easy or interesting,—rhythmically, spatially, by working with a partner.

> For example, walk forward 8 steps while bringing the arms up in front of the body to over the head, walk backward opening the arms to the side and lowering them to the starting position. That's really easy.
>
> Now decrease to 4 steps, speeding up the arms appropriately.
>
> Now do it facing a partner who starts 4 counts later.
>
> Or change directions every 4 steps, not just forward and back but including diagonals, circles, curves while moving the arms on 8 counts for each phase and always returning to the same front.
>
> Even harder, do this facing a partner who starts 4 counts later. The one who starts after 4 counts has to repeat the paths taken by her partner.

By this time there are clouds of smoke from overworked heads.

Talking point: Now is the time to talk about arm coordination, knowing where the arms are, moving them at will, having control. It's also time to leave it and do something completely different but to come back to it somehow before the end of class. A jump across the space with special arm movements, not too complicated but formed, would be a possibility.

6

GROUP AND SOLO IMPROVISATION

Most of the improvisational structures we have discussed in Chapters 2 and 3 are solo improvisations. These are simpler for dance students who are just starting to improvise. It is easier to deal with yourself than with a group of other dancers, no matter how well you know them. Later, solo and group improvisations go hand in hand, especially for children and young people. Both can be used in different ways and with different aims.

Movement invention In a group improvisation, fellow dancers often can help over a dry place, providing impetus when the motor seems to have ground to a halt. It can also jolt a dancer out of movement and thought habits. Conversely, a solo improvisation allows the dancer to pursue movement impulses in depth, following wherever they may lead. This can result in the moment of listening to the body, the sense of "being alone with yourself" which I mentioned in chapter 3 ("Introducing Improvisation").

Integration In groups, improvisation can encourage group consciousness and remove physical and mental barriers between individuals faster and more effectively than discussion or analysis.

Release When a class is very unruly it can help to implement an improvisation that allows them to unload their excess energy. Several teen-age students have told me that they feel better when they retreat into their bedrooms and dance when they are upset or depressed.

Heightened Awareness In a group improvisation the dancers must be aware of their fellow dancers in order to be able to improvise as a group. Each individual member of the group should be clear in her movement so that her fellow dancers see her intent. In solo improvisation, there's nowhere to hide, no respite from concentrating.

Freedom/Adventure/Surprise For youngsters improvisation is the moment to do what you want,—at last! Well, almost.

There are the rules and stipulations set up by the teacher, but inside those limits the choices are enormous. For the dancer and the observer, improvisation becomes an adventure: what do I see? What do I want? What would happen if....? Sometimes the choices lead into unusual situations, or to an unexpected moment that has evolved from the group action. The next step, literally and figuratively—is always a surprise for the viewer and for the dancer/s.

Fun In a youngster's world,—full of do's and don'ts, laws, prohibitions and warnings, doubts, fears and uncertainties—doing what you want to within clear parameters is simply fun. This should never be underestimated or forgotten and is as important for the teacher to remember in her preparation as for the students to experience in class.

Most improvisational structures can be tweaked to accent one or the other area, but rarely fulfill only one. The action takes place on various levels and yields multi-faceted results.

A word about preparation: preparing an improvisation means knowing why you want to introduce the class to this particular material and process, but not necessarily what result you would like to see. If you find a fascinating object to show in class, it helps to analyze why you find it fascinating, then try to find a kinesthetic reaction to it in yourself, an impulse to dance. Once you've found this (and if you don't, you'd better not expect your students to find it) it's easier to translate that into questions for your students, keeping in mind their age and dance experience.

The order in which changes are introduced, at which points the class observes and reflects, what specific questions are asked of the observers give the improvisation focus and structure. These are not things that can be firmly planned ahead of time. To a certain extent you must improvise too. But your preparation will give you a basis for response. (It also helps to ask yourself "what could go wrong" when you are preparing the improvisations.)

On the other hand, it's important that the improvisation provide the students with something that they can see and evaluate. This produces a feeling of accomplishment. Conversely, without understanding what they have been doing and why, we're back to the scarf-waving anarchy I mentioned in the chapter on technique versus creativity. The students will lose interest.

The following broad categorization of sources may also help to keep your improvisation choices varied.

visual aids: things to be looked at
e.g. postcards, reproductions of paintings, photographs, dance videos, masks
tactile/visual stimulants: objects that can be touched and/or set in motion
e.g. plastic drop cloths, feathers, chains, slinky (spiral toy), soft squeaky stuffed animals,
verbal description/texts: poems, descriptions, short texts
e.g. haikus, haunted houses, dream descriptions, proverbs/adages
rules/games: stipulations, limits, alternatives that govern the movement and its variations
e.g. movement chain ('a turn, a fall, a locomotive movement'); if you meet someone, do something; the ceiling is a meter/yard away from the floor
music: using the music as main impulse
e.g. make a movement chain fit other music; which music is she dancing to? dance between the notes

In general, visual aids, tactile/visual stimulants work best with young students, or with older children who are just starting to dance. Verbal descriptions, rules/games and music work better with older and/or more experienced students.

Let's look at some improvisational structures using various sources and investigate the ways they can be tweaked to accent different areas and for different age groups. A clear description of each structure is provided, followed by an "X-ray" showing the reasons (in italics) for the directions given. Hopefully these reasons will help you in structuring and leading your own improvisations in your classes.

Category: visual aids.
Aim: integration.
Age: 8-10 year olds.
Music suggestion: Glass Harp or Tomita plays Debussy: The Sunken Cathedral, very low volume
My process for choosing: this is a happy picture. I like soap bubbles, especially how they move.

My thoughts on "what could go wrong": the movement will be too fast, too general (big fat bubbles racing around and exploding onto the floor). It will degenerate into a game of tag, possibly a violent one. No one will want to be the girl, being a bubble is too much fun. How can I make a group action out of this?

Process: show soap bubble picture.

Ask questions/discuss: where are the bubbles coming from? *make movement and sense of space clear. Prevent racing around.* Is the girl trying to break the bubbles or catch them? *clarification of intent, avoidance of violence.* What's on the ground and what's in the air? *clarify situation, contrast of movement and stillness, levels.* Can you hear a bubble if it lands on the grass? *sensual detail.*

Are the bubbles big or small? *encouragement of variety*

What happens if you touch a bubble too hard? *avoidance of violence, sensual detail.*

How can you touch a bubble without breaking it? *sensual detail*

Try out: phase 1: everyone is a bubble. See if you can land lightly on the floor or on a wall or even on another bubble, making a double bubble. *Get the class moving, initial contact with each other, experimentation.*

phase 2: teacher is the girl, stands still. The bubbles (1/2 the class) float around her. She tries to catch them by touching them very lightly. *No one wants to stand still, but if the teacher does it, it becomes acceptable.*

phase 3: The observers become the bubbles; the group that just tried with the teacher becomes the girls. They cannot move their feet, but try to catch the bubbles with different body parts without breaking them by touching the bubbles gently as they float by. Once touched the bubble can remain attached or float on when the girl moves. *contrast of abridged and free movement, observation of others, freedom of choice*

phase 4: Change groups and add the rule that the bubbles are attracted to the girl and all bubbles must be attached to somewhere on the girl by the end of the improv. *avoidance of element of playing tag (freedom of bubble is not gladly relinquished), building larger groups.*

Reflection: was it harder to be the girl or the bubble? Why? What did you have to be careful of when you were a bubble? A girl?

phase 5: limit the space by drawing chalk lines on the floor or setting up mats or chairs as boundaries. *to shorten time by increasing frequency of meetings*

Everyone is a bubble within the delineated space. *entire class moves* The aim is to build as big a multi-bubble as possible with no broken bubbles. Like the real bubbles, attachment (docking) can happen at any point on the surface of the bubble.

Lots of physical contact and probably laughing. By this time everyone has had physical contact with everyone else—the first step to group integration.

Reflection: How many different body parts were used as attachment places (docking stations)? Was it hard to move as a multi-bubble? Why?

By moving away from the picture in the initial discussion phase, the same source could be used for older students, say 12-14 years, with the aim of movement invention and imagination. Here are the changes along with the "X-ray" and teaching tips:

Category: Visual aids
Aim: Movement invention and imagination.
Age: 12-14 years

My preparatory thoughts: I like this picture, but they will think it's for 'babies'. How can I upgrade it so that they feel challenged on their level?

Ask question, discuss: What's moving in the picture? What's not moving? What couldn't possibly move?

Aim for three categories: free movement—the bubbles; limited movement—the girl; movement impossible—the ground, grass. Be prepared for the argument that the grass moves under foot and in wind, and the earth moves in an earthquake and the bubbles only move when blown. With this age group you can talk about general qualities: a bubble symbolizes freedom; a child, liveliness; the ground and grass, solidity.

What's the difference between a child's movement and that of a bubble? Is one lighter, faster, more varied than the other? What kind of movement did you like to do when you were this age (everyday movement not dance movement)? Hopping? Skipping? Running? Twirling/spinning? Jumping? Rolling? Write down the movement terms on a blackboard or flipchart.

What kind of movement does a bubble "do"? Growing? Bursting? Floating? Turning? Write down these movements in a separate column or section.

Prime the pump to get them going by making suggestions that incorporate several levels and dynamics. Keep you eye on the clock and the class on the subject.

Try Out: phase 1: divide the class into 2 groups, the children and the bubbles. Let each group choose three movements from the appropriate column and link them together to make a movement chain,—one chain for the bubbles, one for the 'children'. Each member of the group dances her own version of the chosen movements. The 'children' and the 'bubbles' show their movement chain to each other.

> At this point you can ask for affirmation or suggestions, but that would entail a second work phase to incorporate suggestions, improve, etc. There's seldom time for this, and often the students lose patience or interest. Or introduce this initial viewing as a 'get-acquainted' phase rather than an evaluation and make it short, with each group standing in place to watch rather than sitting down and becoming the passive viewers.

Phase 2: The children and the bubbles dance simultaneously, with the stipulation that once a child meets a bubble or vica versa a duet takes place, either because they're stuck together, or the child prevents the bubble from escaping (without breaking it), or the child becomes the bubble doing her own movements in a 'bubble' way and integrating them with the bubble movements, or the bubble becomes the child and changes her movement accordingly. Show in smaller groups.

Here we have a little scenario> something happens, changes, and is interactive. If you've run out of time, you already have here a product so that the students have a sense of process leading to product, important for this age level. Don't try to carry this over to the next week if there's no time for phase 3.

Reflection: was the movement change easy to see? Could you always tell who changed? Did they really dance together or was each one doing her own thing? For the dancers: which movement was harder to do—bubble or girl? Was one more enjoyable than the other?

Phase 3: Divide the class in trios. Each trio draws lots to determine who dances what—a) unmoving, b) bubble, c) child. Now we make a movie/video/story: each trio decides what will happen: the unmoving object (a building, a monument, a sign) is planted in the performance space and influences what happens (the bubble could break, the building could fall, the monument could melt, the child could freeze). It could be comedy, a tragedy, a science fiction story. They have to decide what happens and where (on the lawn, in space, in a city, underground, in school etc) and how it ends movement-wise. Give a time limit for the process. A limit of 15 minutes is probably realistic.

The trios rehearse, and then show individually.

This is a long phase but it is the moment where the students can let loose and the bit of imagination used in phase 2 is given free rein. Using words like video, movie make it seem more "grown-up" and contemporary. It also gives them ideas (they've all seen movies). You can help to prime the pump by giving suggestions, especially about what the unmoving object could be and that it can, under circumstances in the story, move.

As you observe the groups make sure that the scenarios stay simple. One change is enough. The more ideas they have ("and then … and then … ") the less clear it is for the observers and the dancers and the longer it takes to think of movements that relate the story. Also make sure they spend more time dancing than thinking about the scenario!

Reflection: Was this more interesting—to dance, to watch—than the previous phase? Why?

Here hopefully the students will realize how important the contrasting movement dynamic is. If they don't come up with it themselves, you may have to prod a bit.

Which part of the process—preparation or showing—was more enjoyable for the dancers? *Plan 10 minutes for this.*

This very long improvisation would be good to use when you sense a certain fatigue in the class or yourself with technique and learning given movement.

Category: visual stimulants
Aim: adventure/heightened awareness
Age: 14-16 year olds

Each dancer lies on the floor in a shape, which is outlined in chalk by another student. If available, use felt pens and unprinted newspaper

The moment of deciding the shape and drawing it makes it more tangible for the youngsters and leaves room for self-determination. If possible draw the figures in a floor space that will remain untouched during the ensuing work.

Divide the class into trios.

If the class is larger than 12, quartets also work.

Each trio chooses 4 shapes and sets the order, which shape is first, second, etc. Each dancer takes responsibility for one shape, developing the movement that leads from that shape to the next shape.

Allows for individuality within clearly defined limits. Depending on the level of the group, the length of the transitional movement can be set, e.g. count of 8 or16 beats.

You give tempo. Otherwise you may be confronted with the shortest distance between two points. A time stipulation prevents this short cut and forces the students to think more about the possibilities.

Base requirement: the group has to move 5 meters from beginning to end of the resulting movement chain.

Involves spatial consciousness.

All do the same movements, learning from each other.

Demands clarity, strengthens communication

When the initial chain is done, the trios draw lots for weather—earthquake, cyclone, hail, thunderstorm, snowstorm, burning heat, and rework the chain showing how this changes tempo, length of each movement, proximity to each other, contact to floor, etc.

The listing of these details helps refine the changes, revealing possibilities.

Each group shows unweathered, then the weathered versions.

Reflection: Which version was more interesting, did you like better? Why? Is it possible to tell which weather was danced? Is it important for your enjoyment to know this?

This last question brings the students out of the heads and into the body, away from literal recognition and toward sensual appreciation and especially encourages them to have confidence in their reactions rather than resorting to intellectual analysis. Coincidentally it discourages the idea of a right and wrong in improvisation. Even if the answer is that recognition is important, it at least raises the possibility of an alternative approach to appreciation.

Category: rules
Aim: Release
Age 6-12 years

If a group is very unruly at the beginning of class, and if you're working in a very large space—a good-sized dance studio or a gym—it can help to let the class run as fast as they can across the length of the space while screaming as loud as they can.

This may sound like a confession of weakness on your part, but it very effectively gets rid of the excess energy and aggression, which can build up during a school day. It does not work for students over 12 because they are (usually) too socialized by that age to really let go. It also will not work in a small space. You'll find that even the quieter students will run and scream—the lure of the forbidden. This also puts everyone in the same position, not good and bad, quiet and loud, cooperative and obstreperous, which is not a bad place to start from.

Category: music
Aim: release, awareness
age: 10 years on

Scatter the students throughout the space and let them put on blindfolds. Assure them that you will watch out for them, preventing collisions, but ask them to remember that there are others dancing in the space. Invite the class to move to the music and assure them that no one can see and you're too busy playing traffic cop to watch them. Put on the music—atmospheric, melodic, ethnic, but not rock or rap as they are too confining. You will definitely be too busy to evaluate their movement.

Reflection: how did it feel? Was it more pleasant to move with blindfolds than without? Could they feel other people? How?

**Category: rules, games. Aim: heightened awareness, music
age 10 (experienced) or 12 years**
Teach the class a combination of at least 4 measures (4 x 8) to rhythmic music. When they have learned it, talk about how the movement fits the music, how the music influences the dance, not just the time, but also the dynamic, the feeling.

Play 3 different music selections for the class. Non-metric, electronic, symphonic are some of the possibilities,—anything that is a contrast to the music to which the combination was learned. Each dancer decides which music she would like to accompany the previously learned combination. (It helps to have one music on tape, the others on CD and to have an additional sound source on hand, a boom box for example.)

The dancers rehearse but not with the music playing constantly. They can listen now and then, but emphasize that they should try not to mirror the music, but to transport its essential quality, without "mickey-mousing" (a cartooning term for a movement on every note).

They must include all the movements from the combination in their learned order.

Before they show, play each of the three music selections once to remind the class of the possibilities. Finally three dancers at a time show without music what they have done. The viewers have to guess who is dancing to which music.

It helps to assign watchers for the showing. If the 3 performers have chosen different music, the viewers need to concentrate on individuals, otherwise it can be confusing.

This can be carried over for a week if the combination has proven more difficult to learn than you expected or planned for. A short review is enough in the second week before moving on to the improvisation.

Reflection: how could you tell which music your dancer was using? Why couldn't you guess which music it was? What do you think could have been done to make it clearer? How did the combination change with the new music?

You should be reaching for adjectives with the last 2 questions. Priming the pump helps:

was it too fast? too percussive? did it make you laugh? sad? or adjectives about the music: like a storm, like a mechanical toy, like a horror movie ...

One of the main aims of this improvisation (and it is one in spite of the learned movement) is finding the musicality of the movement without sitting on the music. For this reason it is very important to choose clearly different, strongly defined music selections and not to let them run constantly as the dancers work. Otherwise there is danger of mickey-mousing, exactly what we're trying to avoid.

Reality Check 12-14 year olds

The class of 12-14 year olds was coming along nicely. They came to class regularly and were engaged by the challenges presented by our teacher. As a result, she thought that a plan for an improvisation structure concentrating on tempo and dynamic changes would not present any problems. The initial phase passed without incident. It required the dancers to experiment with a given combination, taught by the teacher, changing its tempo and movement quality in as many ways as possible. This was danced in groups of threes, with the rest of the class observing. After a discussion of the different qualities and tempi involved and how the combination felt and looked, the teacher asked the whole class to abandon the given combination and to move through the different tempi and qualities which they had used for the given combination, but this time using spontaneous movement ideas. After an experimental phase with the entire class, she asked Suzy, Ingrid and Bettina, three girls who had been with her for 2 years, to show what they had.

The class sits against the wall, the three girls move slowly out to the center of the space as our teacher moves to put on some background music and gives the signal to start. The three look at each other, at the others and remain still. The teacher again calls out "begin", with no noticeable effect. The teacher turns the volume down, and asks what the problem is. The girls fidget, very ill at ease, Ingrid finally mumbles, "It's embarrassing".

The teacher looks quickly at the rest of the class, who are beginning to fidget, look at the ground, whisper to each other and pick at their dance clothes. She grabs a drum and tells the whole class to move to the drum, then she uses a cymbal, an ocean drum, a cachichi, telling them to move appropriately to each sound. Then she divides the class into partners, only one partner can move at a time. When one chooses to freeze in movement, her partner must start. The teacher continues, using different instruments, calling to the class to use their whole bodies, all levels, different body parts, She inserts a non-rhythmic, non-melodic CD (e.g. "Different Trains" Steve Reich) and tells them to continue in partners, using all the choices they had before: levels, body parts, qualities but using their own imagination instead of depending on the instruments. The class moves.

What's happening here?

This age level is often acutely self-conscious and dependent on group judgments. Ingrid, Suzy and Bettina, despite experience and ease in improvisation, were suddenly confronted with being the object of everyone's attention as well as having to move spontaneously. The previous phase, although there was exposure, pro-vided protection through the given movement. That was one thing they were not responsible for. Lowering the volume of the music instead of turning it off is a small detail, but it signaled that activity is not coming to stop. Getting the entire class moving without an "embarrassing" discussion of why it was embarrassing to move, released everyone. The assignment to look at your partner and react to her encouraged observation but not exposure as the entire class was doing it. The use of instruments left some free choice of what movement, but gave guidance for the quality. Freezing in movement maintains concentration. The final use of a sound background, which gave no hints, left the choice of quality and movement free, but without the element of exposure.

7

WHAT MAKES A DANCE?

Interesting movement alone does not make a dance (but it's nice if there is some). Neither do wonderful dancers, beautiful costumes, marvelous music or a fascinating theme. A dance has a beginning, middle and an end. It can be as simple as the lights going on at the beginning and off at the end. Although the viewers may not be happy, it's still a recognizable unit.[1]

Without the establishment of this unit the audience will be dissatisfied or frustrated or angry or bored or disinterested,—not always on a conscious level, but certainly unconsciously. This will affect their judgment and the effect the piece has on them. Most of us have seen pieces in which the dancers dance offstage as the music is faded out. Think back to your feelings when this happened. It usually leaves a sense of incompleteness,—where have they gone? What would have come next? What am I missing? Of course, this can be a conscious decision on the part of the choreographer. But in work with children and young people, one of the reasons for making a dance with them is a pedagogical one: to provide them with the experience of dancing in a piece, not a combination, not a section but an entire piece, with a beginning, middle and end.

It is vital that our choreographer/teacher has an idea of how the piece should end. Equipped with an end, she can work her way back to the beginning and find an appropriate middle. My first ballet teacher said, "Always finish strong, even if you've fallen down". Not bad advice. The ending is what the audience takes home, their last memory of the dance. It can reverse the perceived meaning, intensify it, comment on it, be funny, poignant, touching or stunning, but it should be an end not just a cessation. Whether the dance is 3 minutes long or 30, it always helps to know where you're going.

Once the existence of a unit of presentation is established choice enters the picture,—the choreographer's choice of what's being presented, the viewers' opinion about what they are seeing, etc.

For almost all audiences, the prime requirement of a performance is that something happens. For many people, and especially for children, this means that a story

---

1.   Many experiments have been made, and are still ongoing, about the nature of a dance piece, or even of a performance. In the early 1960's the Judson Church Group questioned the necessity of form, content, visibility, lights, costumes and trained bodies in a dance performance. The development of Performance Art has continued the experimentation. This kind of work certainly has its validity, but it is perhaps out of place with children and should be used with discretion with young people. I think it helps to have mastered, or at least experienced the basic forms, before breaking them. Otherwise youngsters think they have invented the wheel, simply because they are unaware of what has already happened—the history of dance. (Looking at photographs is a good way to introduce them to this, especially if you can explain the contexts. This also provides—for students from 12 years on—in itself a context for dance class, another move away from "baby stuff".)

is told. What many people do not realize is that there is more than one way to tell a story. The body has its own language. A dancer's body has a finer language—more meanings, shadings and more "vocabulary"—than an untrained body. In dance classes, we try to make this vocabulary available to our students. The movement is the medium in class, as it should be for transporting that "something happening" onto the stage.

Unfortunately, when students have one weekly dance class, or even two, which must compete with schoolwork, social development and familial obligations for their concentration, the chance of establishing a finer vocabulary in their growing bodies is often very small.

In addition they are often more sophisticated in their reading, their taste, their verbal abilities than in their physical ones. Think of the 8 year old who shows an improvisation in which nothing much happens physically, and when asked afterward what it was about, goes on for 20 minutes with an extremely complicated verbal explanation filled with "and then.... and then.... and then".

When it comes time to choose the subject of the dance for the next performance, the students' suggestions will often be very far from their physical possibilities. Faced with this dilemma, the choreographer/teacher often reaches for props, spoken text and voluminous program notes, or, if the budget allows, ornate costumes and scenery to transport the "story" or the content suggested by the class.

It is at this very early point, the choice of 'what the dance is about', that the choreographer/teacher makes her choice of medium. She should be the translator, the bridge between the students' suggestions and the world of movement. Only she can be aware of the abstractions necessary to turn these ideas into a viable dance that is possible for the students to perform. Only she can find the moment that could give the idea form,—the 'middle' between the 'beginning' and the 'end'. This moment can be at the end or the beginning, but it has the function of "something happening". If she jumps too soon to text or props, costumes or scenery, they may turn into hindrances for the development of the dance. In the next chapter I will discuss some ways of dealing with this problem.

Beauty versus Story or Can "just dancing" Make a Dance

"Just dancing" is often the wish of older students, teenagers who consider stories something for babies, for children, but not any more for them. Even in this sort of dance, something has to happen.

A dance, which consists of a group performing a series of formations, combinations, and effects remains exactly that,—a series. Like a conversation screamed or whispered all at one level, this sort of 'dance' becomes boring very fast. It's hard for the viewer to order, to find a reference point, to identify what he is seeing. If the middle is suddenly performed in slow motion, or one section is repeated by a soloist, if the space or direction or size of the movement changes,—a form emerges. Any sort of compositional manipulation will help the viewer to differentiate what he is seeing. He can make order out of it, he can remember it.

In dances of "pure" movement the smallest details make a huge difference. If a group is built as single dancers join it, what happens to that group suddenly becomes very important. Does it stay together? Explode into pieces? Separate into smaller groups? It has become a dance <u>about</u> individuals and groups, and in that sense has a story. More importantly, this 'story' has emerged from the movement, not from an element imposed upon it.

Difficult dances to make with children/youngsters:

popular stories ("Harry Potter" etc.), films and cassettes. You'll never make a dance as good as the original story, film or cassette.

subjects with "non-movement" themes (environmental issues, political problems). Yes, you can do a "tree-growing-and-being-chopped-down" dance, but do you want to? And is it about the environment or about a tree growing and being chopped down?

adaptations from classical plays and stories. As in popular stories above—you'll probably never attain the excellence of the original. Usually these are attempts to make these plays and books palatable and understandable to the youngsters. The adaptations should be simplified plays or stories, not dances. John Cranko has made beautiful ballets about "Romeo and Juliet" and "The Taming of the Shrew". But he had the Stuttgart Ballet to work with. More to the point, these ballets are concerned with love, jealousy, fury, tragedy, and anger—good danceable themes. They do not try to transport Shakespeare's language.

Stories that revolve around a solo figure are difficult to rehearse. They also run counter to almost all the ideas in this book. If a teacher has tried to establish a non-threatening atmosphere, to build a community in her classes, casting and rehearsing a dance that revolves around one figure will go very far to destroy that atmosphere and the community. Suddenly dance is all about being the best, pleasing the teacher. Double or multiple casting—having several youngsters dance the princess—doesn't solve the problem. Instead of a chosen one you have a chosen caste. You have re-established competition.

Dances, which seem easy to make with children and young people:

dances to songs: songs with lyrics transport their meaning primarily though the words. The dance takes, at least for the listener/viewer, a secondary role. If a dance is composed to a song with words, the dance is usually an effect, a decoration. The dancers illustrate the lyrics. This dance doesn't exist independently. It cannot stimulate the dancer or the viewer to new insights. It does not touch that non-verbal place in the imagination that dance can touch, whether performed by children, lay people or professionals. (A musically complex song where the movements interact with the musical arrangement, not the lyrics, is an exception.) In musicals and musical theater this is appropriate, but in a dance concert it seems to me a wasted opportunity.

Movement is already an abstraction for many people. If it proceeds without a frame, without a shape, it will make very little impression.

For the performers a dance is like a complete dinner as compared to the appetizer of a combination. Dancers, even young dancers, live the story, live the dance. It is important that they know where the dance is going and why, how it ends and why. The discussions at the beginning of the work help. That is why the question of how to end the dance is important to discuss with the students. In this way, they assume ownership of the ideas, not just the movement. It is another sort of growth, but one that is very necessary.

8

MAKING A DANCE

Let's assume that when you start to make a dance you want to draw the class into the process. Before any discussion with the class, you should know the general framework of the performance (if there is a general theme which should be considered), and where it will take place (performance venue influences the composition of the dance. Young dancers cannot adjust to different performance conditions as quickly as professionals can). These conditions must stay in the back of your mind as you talk with the class.

If there are no overall thematic stipulations, a dance can start from many points, each one with its own demands and its own pitfalls. The pitfalls (in bold) are the specific problems posed by each starting point. The questions are for the teacher/choreographer to ask herself.

Starting from an idea

> How does it make you feel?
> Can you see a development—emotionally, **physically?**
> Can you imagine an end?

Starting from a movement combination

> Why this combination?
> Is it possible to make it **interesting**? How?
> What will the class learn from this? Why?

Starting from a picture

> Whose choice is this?
> Can you help the class not only enjoy and value the picture, but use it as a **creative source? How?**
> Or vica versa—can you understand the class's choice and use it as a creative source?

Starting from music

> Why this music?
> Can you use the whole piece?
> If not, how will/can you manipulate it?
> Is it new, fresh and exciting?
> Does it leave you room to develop **the dance as an equal partner** of the music?

Starting from a text

> Is it a provocative source or a corset? Is it a jumping off place, an inspiration, or a user's manual?
> Does it have structure inherent in it?
> Is it possible to develop one without violating the original text?

Can the resulting dance stand alone without a citation of the text?
If so, does that make the dance weaker or stronger?

Starting from an environment (site specific)

Is it appropriate for the ages you're working with?
What strictures are inherent in the site and **what new opportunities does it offer, movement-wise**?
How will weather effect the performance?
How can you rehearse it in the studio?

Once these questions have been answered and a theme is chosen, it often helps to ask the students how they see the dance: should it be happy or sad, suspenseful, poetic, dramatic or something else. Should the end be a surprise, a logical resolution, a shock? Their answers will help you to form the dance, to decide on the famous beginning-middle-end. It is important to ask as many questions as possible. Imagine a child having been promised a surprise and asking endless questions in an attempt to find out what it is. In this case you are the child. The students have vague ideas and so do you. Questions help everyone to define the idea to a place where work can start.

As you speak with the class about the dance and suggestions come from them, an inner dialogue should be going on in your head. You imagine the possibilities that the suggestions stimulate in you,—the movement possibilities, the look and feel of this subject on stage with these dancers,—and every part of this sentence is equally important.

> It is to be a performative event. No matter what the venue, people will be watching.
> These students, not professionals or older dancers, will dance it.
> The movement development should stem from or reflect the subject.
> In the 'imagined possibilities' mentioned above, is it movement you're imagining or stage effects?
> Can you see a story? A development?

It's at this point that the teacher is the bridge between the students' suggestions and the world of movement. The choreographer/teacher must decide how to develop movement and improvisational structures as well as working toward an over-all form for the dance.

Various stratagems for developing movement and improvisational structures

If the movement is the medium, the first step should be its development and not production choices (music, costumes, props, lights). A few examples, using the starting points listed above:

Starting from an idea:

Possible themes for children older than 10 years: cliques in groups; a wall through a city; social castes or the Other in society. In all these ideas a conflict is inherent. There are 2 different sorts of people involved: the ones in the clique, the ones outside; the ones on one side of the wall, those on the other; the majority and the minority.

What kind of conflicting movement can be developed?

> high versus low?
> spatially adventurous vs. spatially constricted?
> soft, lyrical versus hard, fragmented? etc.

The class, divided in half or groups can develop a movement chain (as in Chapter 7, e.g. a fall, a locomotive step, a turn) using one or the other set of characteristics.
A given movement sequence (that you have taught the class) can be worked the same way.
Both elements,—the given movement as well as the movement chain remain recognizable, providing an element of unity despite the variety of presentation.

Possible themes for children under 10: Christmas cookies; getting lost in the forest. Both ideas involve process, change.

> For cookies, one needs flour, sugar, eggs, baking powder, vanilla, sometimes chocolate, sprinkles, nuts. All these ingredients have a particular consistency, in dance terms a particular movement dynamic.
> When they are blended, yet another consistency/dynamic evolves, when they are baked, they change shape, and when they are eaten they transform themselves into a big tummy. Plenty of material there for improvisation.

> Getting lost in the forest can involve trees,—helpful or hindering, bushes, animals, possibly spirits, and other lost people.

The process—carefree start (fast, light, airy) mounting fear (constriction, hesitant movement), happy end (release and return to fast, light and airy).

Starting from a movement combination

This can be a combination that the class has already learned and likes (caution: boredom) or one that poses technical challenges which can only be mastered over a long rehearsal period, with the coming performance providing the incentive and preventing boredom.

This source is really a test of the choreographer/teacher's ingenuity: how many different ways can the combination be manipulated? Can it be danced backwards (retrograde) upside down, with other body instrumentation, fragmented, in slow motion, on different levels?

But still there is room for improvisation:

> each dancer chooses her favorite parts and links them together, leaving out the bits she doesn't like;
> each dancer takes two of her favorite movements and makes them even more pleasing to herself, changing levels, timing and dynamic at will;
> two dancers change the order of the movements, retaining all of them in this combination. One of the partners performs the new combination while her partner echoes her, or fills the spaces left empty by the movement, or performs them in a contrasting level, dynamic, time or with other body parts.

The possibilities are close to endless. This choice is usually made by older students. By letting them leave out the bits they don't like, their personal taste is satisfied. By offering new improvisational approaches, their horizon is broadened.

Starting from a picture or other visual art

Very often during the process of choosing the picture, whether it happens with or without the class, words come up which can be very helpful for finding movement. Mostly these words are adjectives describing feeling and impressions caused by the picture. Melancholy, lonely, angry, pensive, electrifying, pitiful, sly, funny (I am thinking here of paintings by Klee, Kiefer and Matisse, objects by Bruce Naumann, photos by Diane Arbus, WEEGEE). These adjectives can influence the tone, the over-all mood of the dance.

Movement invention can come from a variety of other sources:

> the subject matter:

swimming fish (Klee),
coverings which are full then empty, (Kiefer)
the twists involved when dancers in a circle hold hands but perform
individual movement (Matisse).

> the colors or medium employed:

are they harmonious or conflicted?
suggestive of other places, times or events?

> spontaneous connections/reactions in the viewer's imagination.

> imagining what happened just before or just after the moment in the
picture.

The interesting thing about working with visual images, at least for me, is that it
is similar to dance. Working from an image is a very non-verbal affair.

Starting from music

If you are working from a specific piece of music it helps to analyze its musical
form, just to know its patterns and timing (not the rhythm, but the length of
time the sections take.) One could call this musicality.

>If the piece of music has a specific atmosphere, you can discuss that
feeling with the class, then
>leave the music and improvise on that mood or situation without
music or using other music.
>Once the movement is established, you can go back to the chosen
music and rehearse with it, always maintaining the dance form that has
been developed.

Children and young people are amazingly responsive to music. In the process
described above they will begin to find the musicality of the music without giving
up the musicality of the movement. This process can often develop the musicality
of the youngsters faster and more efficiently than "dancing to the music" can.
Although the initial shock may be great, they will understand the feeling, the
musicality, the tension in the dance better and in addition will have learned to be
flexible.

Dances for children and young people, especially in a studio or school performance situation, are limited by the amount of rehearsal time available. Three
minutes of movement take a very long time to develop and perfect. Interesting
pieces of music which are three minutes long are hard to find. Collages often
seem to be the solution to this problem.

Music collages should be handled with extreme caution. Mickey-mousing the
movement by means of the music is as bad as mickey-mousing the music in the
movement.

In the first case, a short section of easily recognizable music, or a song with
text is played under movement in order to clarify the movement's message. In the
second case a high note gets a high movement, fast notes—fast movement, low
notes—dancers on the floor. This sort of choppy sound accompaniment is nerve-
wracking and distracting. The viewer starts to listen to the music for cues about
the movement instead of experiencing the movement on its own merits.

If you must use a collage, it helps to have a very musical sound engineer to
assemble the collage for you.

Very regular, rhythmic music becomes boring, offering no highlights or cli-
maxes, even though it helps the students to find cues easily and to count. It is better not to use music that has been used in class. It seldom holds its interest over a
longer rehearsal period.

Starting from a text

A text usually tells a story,—something happens. That's the good part. A dance
can tell the story in its own language,—movement. First questions for the choreographer should be:

> why do you like this text?
> Is this element danceable?
> How much would be lost in translation from language to movement?
> What could be gained?

Once you have defined what it is you, or your students, find attractive in the text,
you can work from there. Very often, the process is similar to the one described
in "starting from a picture".

It's important to remember that you are not doing the movie version. Very
often children and young people see themselves 'in the story' or even more often
'in the movie'. This is their motivation for choosing it. If the class insists on a
dance about a story/film/book you must find the danceable parts and make it

clear to them that the dance does not have to remain slavishly bound to the text, to its events, to its sequence.

During the process of making the dance, the class usually becomes interested in the process, in the movement and its possibilities. It will become clear to them that they are developing something different, that dance is a different animal from text.

Starting from an environment (site specific)

Older students, from 12 on, can find it "grown-up" to be out of the studio. They find it a challenge to think about the dance possibilities of a new venue—. an interesting stairway, a train platform, a market square. Usually their concentration onsite increases. Faced with a multitude of distractions, they must become very concentrated on what they are doing. This assumes that they have been engaged in the choice of venue, and understand the reason for performing in it. It is up to the choreographer/teacher to find the dance possibilities inherent in the space. These can be developed in the studio, providing the dancers are reminded of the venue conditions.

Here are some possibilities and non-possibilities:

Venue	possible	not possible
a large stairway	levels, appearing/disappearing	floor rolls
market square	mirroring passersby, slow motion	leaping, flailing arms
busy street	zebra stripe: approaching/retreating and mirroring passersby, slow motion kneeling	falling, rolling,
escalator	meeting/parting, going against the direction riding the rolling banisters	as in street
columns in hall	appearing/disappearing separated body parts climbing, hanging	depends on location and size of columns

Getting younger children accustomed to a studio or dance space environment is difficult. Moving into a new, unusual space for a performance with children under 12 is a challenge that brings few rewards.

The step toward the next step/Working toward a Form:

What happens to the initial idea, how does it change (the middle), is the next thing to think about. This can evolve out of the preliminary discussions with the students. Knowing the overall atmosphere as well as how the dance should end can help with movement development and with forming the dance as a whole.

Just as a movement sequence should have a form, so should the dance as a whole, not only a beginning-middle-end but also a build-up to a highpoint and a denouement. The climax can come at any time, even at the end of the dance, followed by a freeze and a blackout. It depends on what serves the idea of the dance best. If you are using the idea of "Lost in the Forest" for example, the climax might be when the children find their way out (end) or when they meet a particularly dangerous animal. The important thing is to know that these are aims to work toward. They serve as plateaus that can help structure your work and your timing—both the timing of the rehearsals and the timing of the piece.

Without this mental outline the work may seem to be proceeding well, but at one point you are lost. How to go on? How to end? Often one is struck with an initial idea that seems fascinating, rich, provocative, stimulating. The first rehearsals roll along; improvisational structures yield interesting results; given movement works well. Suddenly one is confronted with either the problem of development (I'm treading on one place, not moving ahead) or the end (my time is up, how shall we finish).

It is not difficult to stimulate and develop movement. Some ideas for this were discussed in the previous section ("Starting from ..."). However, finding the stimulus that fits the idea of the dance and steering it in the right direction is difficult. Very often, what the students have done is so lovely, it seems wrong not to include it in the dance. If you don't have an overview, these sections can very often lead the dance astray. When the dance consists of walking from one dance section to another, you are fragmenting the dance form, stopping its flow and diminishing its impact on the audience.

In addition, your young dancers have not experienced a form. How many times in class have you told the class to finish the combination, even if the time or space are at an end? This is the beginning of form. If the dance is not formed, the students may have experienced a performative moment, but that is all. The dance has missed its theme—a judgment your older students know all too well from English class. Ordering ideas in dance is just as important as it is anywhere else. It is a general learning goal that can be approached in dance class just as well as in school.

The Old and The New

When I studied dance in the Fifties, form was writ large. Louis Horst taught classes in Pre-Classic and Modern Forms, with very strict compositional rules based on the musical forms. Classical modern dance (as choreographed by Martha Graham, Doris Humphrey, Jose Limon) was understandable in its form, if not in its vocabulary. Though I am tempted to refer to these rules as 'Alphabet Soup' and am not aware of having ever consciously applied them, I must admit that very often, when a dance is finished, I recognize that my early training is still there and has once more emerged to help me. These forms can be useful, especially in work with children and young people. For that reason, and if you are unfamiliar with this way of thinking about dance making, here is a short version[1]: The most common forms are AB and its close cousin AB'

> ABA and its close cousin ABA'
> Theme and Variations
> Rondo ABACADAEAF ...

---

1.   see "The Intimate Art of Choreography" by Chaplin & Blom for a more extensive treatment.

Using our examples from "**Starting from Ideas**":

> Cliques, walls, social castes etc. could be AB or ABA'
>
>> The different groups are represented onstage A; they meet and mix B
>> Or they meet and change only slightly, remaining separate ABA'
>> Or a rondo form: the "different" or separated state (A) is danced
>> between various smaller group encounters (B, C, D, E, F etc)
>
> Cookies: the individual ingredients are presented (A), they are mixed
> and baked (B)
> Lost in the forest: the children set out (A), they get lost, encounter
> adventures (B), find their way out (A')

"Starting from movement combination":

A small group presents it facing upstage (A); the movement is changed spatially, in its timing, etc. (B); the entire group presents it (A')

A trio presents the combination, duos and soli present their versions, the entire group presents the combination—theme and variations

A more recent approach was triggered by the work of Pina Bausch. This work, as it has trickled down to other dancers, choreographers and teachers, consists of setting a situation or a question before the dancers and letting them improvise. With well-trained and experienced dancers, this can produce fascinating results. Knitting these scenes into a whole is an immense challenge, one that very, very few choreographers can meet. In addition, these improvisations are usually solo improvisations. Very few children or young people are willing to improvise alone in class, never mind onstage in performance. For this reason, most of the improvisational structures used here are group structures.

Even using this approach, in order to avoid the "walking between the sections" mentioned above, it is vital to have an overview before you start the actual work. This should help in aiming the improvisation, choosing the questions you want to ask. The results may not be the final form, but it is closer to the mark. It gives you something tangible to work with.

Reality Check—the Choreographer/Teacher

It's time again for the annual performance. Our teacher is sitting with her favorite class,—10-12 year olds who have been with her for two years,—discussing possibilities for the dance. The class is not immediately caught by any of the suggested ideas: Life in the Future, Travels and Trips.

One girl wants to do 'something really hard', another says, "It should be funny", another "Could we have really nice costumes this time?" another "No solos". A more reasonable voice, "Some who want to, could do solos and the others, not". "Let's do a really fast, hot dance". This seems to meet with everyone's approval, everyone except the teacher who sees creativity going down the drain as visions of MTV fill her students' heads. Suggestions for music deepen her depression. Finally our teacher says that she will bring in three or four different choices for music to the next class.

Knowing that she can only work with music that she likes, our teacher, now choreographer/teacher chooses dance music from Cuba (probably too energetic for these youngsters), Asian Fusion with a rhythm base (probably too unfamiliar) and drum music by Tambours du Bronx (certainly fast but with dramatic overtones). All the choices are rhythmic and fast. Whether or not they are 'hot' enough is something the class must decide. Before she plays the choices to the class, she allows herself to explain the reasons for her choices, without exerting influence, at least not blatantly. She emphasizes that this is to be onstage and not on the dance floor at a party. The class chooses the Cuban dance music. "Ooops", thinks our choreographer/teacher, "now what?"

The music has no climax; or rather it's one climax after another. Any development will have to come from the movement. She decides to use meter and rhythm as a theme and to break down the cliques in the class through the use of a rondo form. Over the next 4 weeks she develops a movement chain with sharp focus changes, accents and half- and double-time parts which the whole class learns. This is the 'A' part of the rondo. Next she divides the class into twos and threes, carefully mixing the cliques. She asks each group to find favorite movements which are not in the rondo theme (jumping? turning? falls or slides?) and to make a movement chain out of these that both/all partners can do together, in halftime and in double time.

By this time she is fascinated with what her students have chosen. Ideas generate spontaneously about how she can develop the movement and what direction the dance could take. The students are interested in the movement challenges and the timing and have forgotten that they are working with 'someone else'. They engage critically, constructively and enthusiastically in their own and in their classmates' ideas. Inertia resulting from a lack of ideas is overcome by working on concrete problems. The class and the teacher are swept up in the excitement of making a dance.

What's happening here:

When a teacher is lucky she gets caught viscerally right from the beginning by the ideas the students have discussed. Her imagination gets working and she has fun—a bit like the renewal that happens during improvisation. The involvement is absolute, like working with professionals. That's when she's lucky. For the other times, she can try to use a back door.

For me this is often the craft, the "how to" of dance making. Sometimes I get caught in the challenges of movement manipulation, dynamics, variety, development and climax. Sometimes I have used a problem in the class: problems of integration (cliques), as in our example, the "princess complex" (the student who thinks "I'm better than everyone else" and lets it show) or technical problems (dance technique) as a way of 'priming the pump' These concerns,—for the way movement is worked and the way the dance is shaped,—can provide the push down the road to creativity. Hard to describe, this level of involvement becomes a visceral one, not an intellectual one, though it starts that way.

Creative excitement is ephemeral, magical, illusive. The writer Michael Frayn has called it "… the essential bit—the gadget that makes it all work, the crystal, the chip, the formula, the dodge, the wheeze, the scam, the flick of the wrist, the twist of the fingers, the whatever it is…." ("The Trick of It"). Dealing with the nuts and bolts, the craft can sometimes make that excitement happen. It can serve as the back door into the banquet when you've misplaced your invitation.

9

DANCE IN PUBLIC SCHOOLS

The status quo—an overview

Although dance has always had its place in theaters, community centers and even in churches, it has seldom been an integral part of the public school program. Judged either too elitist or too abstract, it was relegated to after-school activities, civic programs or private dance studios.

Starting in the 1980s arts curricula, which included dance, were established in many English-speaking countries in an attempt to broaden education. Elsewhere school administrators and teachers became aware that growing immigrant populations and increasing numbers of overweight, under-active students were not being served by traditional gym classes or traditional curriculum. In the hope of overcoming aggression, xenophobia and of increasing fitness in their students, these school administrators began to "import" dance and dancers into the schools.

In both cases, educators and administrators more accustomed to traditional tests, scores, grades and achievements, often insisted on outcome-based programs as tangible evidence of activity. They accepted somewhat skeptically the qualities of self-reliance, creativity, and self-realization as by-products of the aims of broader based educational aims, social integration and fitness in what were often under-funded or short-term programs.

Personnel proved to be an additional problem. Which to choose: teachers with a strong education background and some dance knowledge or dance teachers with some teaching experience and in-depth knowledge of dance or performers as artists-in-residence who bring the magic of the art into a school situation? All of these have been tried with varying degrees of success.

Artists-in-residence are here today and gone for the rest of the school year. A dance teacher, eager to get a foot in the door of the public educational process, agrees to produce a performable result within a (usually very short) period of time. She pulls her rabbit out of the hat, produces the show and…. moves on to the next class project to begin again from the beginning.

Class teachers, forced to prepare and present all subjects, often lack time, resources and depth of knowledge for preparation of a creative dance experience for their students. They are forced to rely on recipes,—models offered at workshops, in publications or what they remember from their dance training (usually 2-3 courses offered within a 4 year degree program) to produce some sort of performable dance product,—and this year after year.

This is a good way to produce teacher burnout in short order.

Collaterally, because the class had so much fun performing and the principal, the teacher and the parents were so delighted with the result, the class starts a new project in the following term or school year. Faced with students who now have performing experience but few additional skills, the dance specialist or the teacher has to dig deeper into his/her bag of choreographic tricks/techniques to give the dancers, the audience and the teachers the impression—and it is only an impression—that progress has been made.

It is a mistake to think that youngsters want a quick solution. Think of the hours break-dancers spend perfecting their moves. It's not the students who want a quick result. It's the administrators and teachers.

The Point of Performance

Although dance is a performing art, I think it is misguided to make a performance the first aim of a dance course. In art and music classes, certain skills must be acquired before public exposure. An exhibit or a concert is given only when a certain amount of work has been done, skills achieved, processes worked through.

Performance is a test. But if one does not test a student at the beginning of a course in mathematics, chemistry, French etc. (except for placement purposes), why should a performance be the first goal in a dance course? The dance specialist, like the chemistry, math or French teacher, knows what must be accomplished before her students should be put to the test. Educators and administrators do not have this knowledge and seize on the one thing they know—"the show"! Letting them set the goal is denying one's own expertise, substituting the performative experience for the experience of dance.

Trying to make dance class palatable through the carrot and stick method of dangling the performance as an incentive to achieving skills or to overcome the repetitions of rehearsals will only make the students more impatient. The students, usually practiced at getting through with the least amount of effort, are quick to understand where the carrot is. "Is this in the dance?" becomes the constant refrain. That is the only curiosity aroused. The performative moment is the only goal. The students learn only the minimum about dance and dancing—enough to get through the test.

Although much of the work being done in the schools in these outcome-based programs is outstanding, does it introduce students to dance as a process, an art, a discipline or only to performance?

A Proposal for the future
What can dance—creative, contemporary dance specifically—give to students within a traditional school structure?

The physicality of movement of and by itself is the immediate and most important experience—without the competition involved in gym classes, and without a task to perform (using movement to demonstrate the movement of the planets around the sun or the structure of a sentence etc.). This experience brings the students into their own bodies and, through the creative work on which creative/contemporary dance is based, provides a source of empowerment and a stronger sense of self.

Who's the Teacher?

I refer to the dance teacher within the school environment as a dance specialist. Movement can be used as a tool in almost any school subject: learning sentence structure, math, geography, physics, chemistry[1]. A class teacher with a modicum of dance training can 'use' dance this way, but this is not to be confused with teaching dance itself. For that a professional is needed: a trained dancer with teaching experience or a dance pedagogue who has completed professional training as such. Both have the wealth of knowledge, experience and passion for dance that only a professional can have. It is this knowledge, physical, aesthetic and intellectual knowledge, which authorizes the dance specialist as an expert in the very critical eyes of the students.

Learning Goals

Physical:

> The expansion of physical experience: moving in new and different ways, using imagery to stimulate imagination and physical reaction. "Must" (be faster, throw farther, recite more facts, follow orders) is replaced by "could", potential movement possibilities are revealed and can be explored.
>
> Using space in a different way: spatial arrangements change so rapidly that everyone is continually confronted by new neighbors, spatial inhibitions and freedoms. If there is no 'back' to the class, no physical order of excellence or participation, a new equality is established, allowing all students to participate actively and discouraging passive behavior. Customary expectations, social interactions and behavioral patterns in the class are disrupted. The students experience classmates and the space in a new way.
>
> Achievement of age-appropriate movement skills: Students can develop a vocabulary of skilled movement, based on their individual abilities. This in turn, provides a sense of achievement and increases self-esteem. The curricula (Appendix 1) provide a guide for developmentally suitable skills.

---

1.   See bibliography for books using this approach

Acquaintance with varied movement dynamics, rhythms: improvisational games stimulate unexpected movements in the students, using the imagination as a bridge. The use of theme-appropriate music exposes students to different musical experiences.

Creative:

Ability to improvise: clear and non-threatening structures enable all students to move spontaneously.

Working acquaintance with basic forms: the process of showing improvisations which have a precisely described purpose and discussing these with the students (see chapter on Group and Solo Improvisation) can lead to the understanding that dance is a means of communication, and that the form the dance takes influences its impact on the viewer. (See the chapter on Composition)

Ability to choreograph a short piece on a chosen theme: the choice of theme and of movement suitable for it brings the student to a tactile understanding of the process of presenting an idea. No different than writing an essay, choreographing brings all skills into play,—improvising, forming, communicating, and performing—and transforms the dancer into a creator, an active participant not a passive recipient. This experience of empowerment—not only performing, but creating the dances in which they perform—is perhaps the most beneficial contribution to the students' education that creative/contemporary dance can make in a school environment.

Cognitive:

Some knowledge of dance history, development: placing dance within an historic context, through pictures, slides or demonstration (by the dance specialist or a guest) makes dance real for the students, less exotic. It is easier for them to understand their own experiences placed in a continuum rather than as an isolated experience.

Experience of professional dance productions, optimally live (performances, lecture demonstrations), or through videos, films etc. Most youngsters do not experience dance except on MTV. The opportunity to see skilled dancers performing can stimulate their own ambition and widen their understanding of dance as a medium of expression. Discussing the performances with the dance specialist later can sharpen their critical abilities. By introducing the idea of dance as a profession, of professional training, it broadens their outlook in general and their perception of dance in particular.

Grading: a pass—no pass grading system should be used.

Additional benefits:

Diminish competition—competition for grades, for attention, for excellence, is scaled back. It is not about being best in class (or worst), performing the movement perfectly, but experiencing it, being able to express that experience and later, in improvisation and dance-making, to use it.

Through the sovereignty granted the student, authoritarian roles are dissolved. The dance specialist is no longer the sole giver of information.

The class teacher, either observing or participating, sees her students in a new light, quite literally from a new angle. She can observe how group dynamics change, how individuals respond to individual challenges.

The dance specialist: Dancers are exotic. Learning to accept these exotic beings in the school environment helps to integrate other 'exotics'—those with headscarves, wheelchairs, different skin color or eye shape.

But beside this, or perhaps because of it, the dance specialist crosses borders that class teachers cannot. Her working clothes, her movements, her physical proximity to the students disturb traditional attitudes and force students to evaluate this new teacher and the subject she teaches on a new basis and to re-evaluate their own role in the school.

Notes for the dance specialist: Content and teaching practice

The dance specialist cannot use the exercises and structures she knows from her own training. A whole new set of structures is necessary to

> get the students moving
> make the students aware of what they're doing, its terminology, and delivering standards
> enable the students to improve physical and creative skills

>get the students moving
Any of the structures suggested in the chapter on the first 10 minutes will facilitate work in the public schools. Provide simple directions; use good, lively music and an unstructured use of space.

Try to avoid circles as a constant. A circle builds a sense of group, but it directs the concentration away from what's happening in the body to what's happening in the group. At the beginning of the class, it's important to give the students this 'privacy' of experience.

The more the dance specialist participates,—shakes and freezes an arm, leg or her face—the more permission is given to the students to do so. After all, if the 'teacher' does it, it can't be wrong.

Offer a variety of dynamics, supported by music, as well as movement possibilities in clear structures, which allow the students some choice. Reinforce their choices with positive, encouraging comments.

>**make the students aware**

Give precise conditions for improvisational structures. Remind the observers of the conditions. Keep reflection impersonal (see Chapter 6: Group and Solo Improvisation).

>**enable the students to improve**

Use varied approaches to technical and creative assignments. (see Chapter 5: Increasing technical skills, and Chapter 6)

As the class continues to work the dance specialist gradually introduces more complex structures, enabling more subtle gradations and physical discoveries. Through positive enforcement she encourages the students to trust their own judgment, at the same time making them aware of aesthetic standards. It is not a question of whether an improvisation is good or bad, but whether it fulfilled the conditions (e.g. showed contrasts in dynamic or transferred to two other levels) or not. As the class is exposed to more work, sees videos, experiences each other's work, they become aware of dance as an art, with its own standards.

Skill and knowledge increase as the class progresses. The students are able to create their own work, reflecting their own interests and abilities.

Qualified praise, positive enforcement, achievable goals and varied approaches are even more necessary in schools than in a studio environment. They can provide gratification and incentive when judiciously applied. Students should realize that dance has its own process. Gradually increasing the demands, complicating the structure arouses curiosity. Students watch each other to see how the others solve the problem. Bringing learning materials (flowing textiles, balancing birds,) for improvisation helps. Bringing a musician (drummer, flutist, guitarist) to class opens more than their ears.

More than a chance for dance—a model: This cannot be accomplished in a 4 to 8 week project, or a one-week intensive. It requires continuity.

Optimally creative dance should be taught by a dance specialist weekly in the first four grades, alternating with gym/sport for the entire school year, so that the students experience physical movement twice every week in the school schedule. From the fifth grade on, it should be offered as a choice, either gym or dance.

At the end of each year in every grade, a performance should take place, showing the students' own work and an ensemble piece set by the dance specialist. Ideally all dance classes would appear in one performance, allowing them to see each other, gauge improvement, develop models and see other possibilities.

This sort of program requires massive changes in educational standards for athletics, as well as in the attitude of administrators, principals and teachers.[2] Once these changes have been accomplished, this model can offer students the chance to choose dance on the basis of experience,—not because of social pressures, prejudice or preconceptions,—increasing their movement vocabulary, knowledge and respect for the art form and its discipline, as well as respect for themselves and the people around them, whether students or teachers.

A "Dancing Head" for me includes a mobile mind, an open heart, and communication channels open to the entire body. Dance class, whether in school or at a studio, should keep these channels open, allowing physical and intellectual knowledge to move through the body as the body moves through the world.

---

2.   Many countries are already working in this direction. New York City has completed "A Blueprint for Teaching and Learning in the Arts: Dance"(www.nycenet.edu/projectarts/Pages/A-Curr.htm); National Standards for Dance Education-What Every Young American Should Know and Be Able to Do in Dance (www.aahperd.org or www.ndeo.org for current revisions of the Standards); Arts Council of Great Britain: National Resource Centre for Dance. Personally, I feel the amount of standardization involved here is antithetical to creative/contemporary dance, resulting in a reliance on formulae, rather than on the training, knowledge and experience of the dance specialist.

APPENDIX A
Curricula for ages 4-16

The Curricula were developed over a period of 10 years during several teachers' courses, which I directed in the Tanz Tangente, Berlin. They present the situation at each age in the areas of physical, social, dance and creative (improvisation/ forming) development as well as teaching goals for the ages 4 through 18. The examples of lesson activities indicate age-appropriate approaches and outline possible levels of increased technical aims. They do not constitute a complete lesson plan. Exercises for younger students can of course be repeated for older age groups. All the examples originated at the Tanz Tangente in the children's and young people's classes taught by Elke Buckow, Christiane Kiki Grunz, Beatrice

Krath, Claudia Lehmann, Iris Richter, Nadja Raszewski, Claudia Schadt and by me.

4-6 years

A. How they are; developmental preconditions/where they're at
I. Physical elements:
a. short limbs

b. baby tummy

c. s-form spine

d. unarticulated feet

e. natural turn-in

f. high energy

g. sudden fatigue/exhaustion

h. short concentration span

II. Dance elements:
a. jumping, hopping, running

b. fast, expansive movements

c. simple rhythmic patterns

d. go to floor with ease

e. copy without analysis

f. bad arm/leg coordination

III. Improvisation/forming:
a. are able to improvise easily spatially rather than movement-concentrated

b. have difficulty remembering movement patterns

c. prefer to improvise alone rather than with others

d. very direct and concrete in their actions

IV. Social characteristics
a. very dependent on teacher

b. self-centered, little feeling for group

c. curious

B. What they like/preferences
I. Physical elements:
a. running

b. all forms of jumping

c. rolling etc. on the floor

d. climbing

e. all motoric activity
II. Dance elements:
a. hopping, jumping
b. fast movements
c. turning, spinning
d. balancing
e. level changes
f. clear dynamic contrasts
1. stop/go
g. movement-filled structures and games
III. Improvisation/forming:
a. Imaginary situations and characters (make-believe)
b. showing off
c. dancing a story
IV. Social characteristics
a. would rather work alone than with a partner or in a group
b. demand constant attention from teacher
c. regularity, group rituals

C. Teaching aims: what they should learn and how (class activities)

I. Physical elements:

a. strengthening feet, improving foot articulation
>play the piano with your toes on the floor, without lifting heels
>Catching ants for your anteater: ants are caught under curled toes and walked over to a receptacle.
> smiley heels—teacher draws smiley face with ballpoint pen on Achilles tendon. Students make the face vanish (point toes) and reappear (flex)

b. improve leg articulation
>marionette—the students lift their legs using their hands to manipulate imaginary strings

c. improve consciousness of spine as whole
>rolling down upper body, saying hello to others through stretched legs.
> tiny man climbs down from the crown of the head to the coccyx and back up again without sliding (the teacher creeps with two fingers along the spine, then the students do it in partners)

d. awaken consciousness of individual body parts
>pot of color: foot is dipped into imaginary color and then draws designs. Other body parts can be used e.g. coccyx, elbow, head

e. strengthen stomach and back muscles
>"I lie down …"—on the floor, rolling progressively further down with each addition and waking up in between ("… on my bed, under my nice soft quilt, with my teddy, in my warm pajamas", etc.)
>"bye-bye, hello" on mats on floor, sitting with crossed legs at front edge of mat holding corners, rock onto back (disappearing behind mat) saying 'bye-bye'; roll back to sitting saying 'hello!'

II. Dance elements:

a. hopping on 2 and on 1 leg alternately
>shoe store—walking in different sorts of shoes (high heels, rubber boot, clogs, baby shoes, etc.)

b. hard and soft as dynamic contrasts
>inflating yourself like a balloon and floating away until a bird pecks at you and you collapse to floor

c. awaken consciousness of form
>running alternating with making shapes: a stone on floor, a stork, a windmill, a tree in the wind
>three fields—studio is divided into 3 fields of different consistencies to move through e.g. swamp, deep snow, hot sand; or desert heat, under-water, hurricane

d. space paths: zigzag, diagonal, S-curves, walking backwards
>running in patterns (airplanes in figure 8's) moving through chocolate sauce

e. strengthen rhythmic consciousness
>drumming food or names: mashed potatoes, vegetables with gravy, Veronica, Maybelle Ann, etc.
>divide group in half, one group claps 'apple", the other 'apple tree"; one half claps and says sternly "What is it you've done?" the other innocently "nothing"

f. side gallop
>facing a partner, holding hands gallop side-ways through space, repeat back to back

g. skipping
>'treasure chest'—group moves through room doing 4 skips, then four jumps (2 feet). Later jumps form a square: students jump on each corner but remain facing front. (Saying, "4 skips forward" on skips; "my own treasure chest" on each corner will help)

III. Improvisation/forming:

a. introduce working with a partner
> airplane and pilot: running in curves in partners, arms wide, holding hands, the 'pilot' runs forward, steering the 'plane', who runs backwards
>"To and away" partners face each other holding back (upstage) hands and gallop sideways through space, alternating facing to each other and away from each other

b. audio training
>running to music-freezing, or making shapes on silence
>run with music/on silence move to instrument
>all rhythmic games

c. awareness of beginning/end as concept
>running and freezing (stop and go)

IV. Social characteristics

a. strengthen consciousness of group
>Making a circle at the beginning and end of class as ritual (clapping/ stamping etc.)
>stand in circle, a huge one, a tiny one etc

b. encourage tolerance and consideration
> airplane and pilot: s. above
> learning to move through the space in rows of threes

c. encourage cooperation
> islands—place hoops on floor, as many hoops as students. Run on music, on stop jump into a hoop (island) but only one student per island

In the following curricula, class activities become more complex and refer to several of the outline points at once. Therefore I have separated the class activity section from the outline points A., B. and C. and used the traditional

sections "warm-up", "standing technique and floor work" and "center" or "moving through space" to classify these activities.

6-8 Years

A. How they are; developmental pre-conditions, where they're at
I. Physical elements
a. growth phase in limbs
b. s—form spine
c. more conscious control of feet, hands, more refined mobility there
d. knee joint often instable due to growth spurt
e. like to run, jump
f. increased concentration span
g. much physical energy
h. undefined whole-body consciousness

II. Dance elements
a. fast, angular movements
b. jumps
c. go to floor with ease
d. more conscious control of arm movements
e. observe more consciously

III. Improvisation/forming
a. curious, easily interested (pictures, music, stories, objects)
b. more sophisticated reactions to music
c. recognize beginning-middle-end as principle

IV. Social characteristics
a. enthusiastic, but not uncritical
b. strong relationship with 1 friend
c. sensitive to fairness in all relationships
d. less emotionally dependent on teacher

B. Needs, what they like
I. Physical elements
a. running, jumping, moving to the point of exhaustion
b. like playful forms
c. enjoy using skills, showing accomplishments,
d. repetition

II. dance elements
a. relaxation games

b. enjoy falling, rolling, jumping

c. spinning

e. appreciate order in class structure

III. Improvisation/Forming

a. want to express their ideas

b. assume different roles with ease

c. like stories

d. enjoy experimenting

e. have many ideas/are creative

f. like to work with "best friend"

IV. social characteristics

a. need appreciation of own individuality

b. need trusted partner (teacher, best friend)

c. appreciate fairness, but do not always act fairly

d. like to perform, show

C. Teaching Aims

I. Physical elements:

a. give movement assignments clear structure

b. prevent postural weaknesses

c. differentiate and deepen physical, sensual perceptions

d. preserve joint flexibility

e. strengthen muscles

f. increase torso mobility

II. Dance elements

a. clarify consciousness of knee position (bent/straight)

b. triplets (down, up, up)

c. turns from foot to foot (3-step)

d. space circles, curves

e. going to and from floor

f. placement, introduction of balance

III. Improvisation/Forming

a. emphasize difference between pantomimic and dance elements

b. emphasize working in groups of twos and threes

c. deepen reflection phase

d. make wide palette of possible themes available

e. engagement with sound, rhythm, instruments

f. use of teaching aids

IV. social characteristics

    a. maintain justifiable, clear class structure

    b. reinforce open, tolerant attitude between students

    c. strengthen class/group consciousness

    d. support self-confidence as dancers

Class Activities

Warm-up

    a. running games:

        1. run like animal in circus

        2. on stop run to child whose name is called and move (or stand) as she does

        3. on stop make shape as puppet, strings are cut one by one, puppet ends on floor

        4. run on different ground surfaces (ice, mud, hot sand, etc.)

        5. negative space: prepare 5 chalk circles for a class of 12, all run to music, on gong shapes are made in chalk circles (one child per circle, others continue running). "empty'" spaces in shape are filled by another child using all body parts, then original shaper is free to join runners.

        6. class stands in circle one body part is pulled by magnet in center of circle; then another body part is pulled by magnet outside of circle, (teacher initiates)

Standing technique:

1. roll down upper body with straight knees, crawl out on hands, forming "table" or bridge over puddle) with outstretched body, crawl back, roll up.

2. carrying sand sack on head while walking, during plies, leg swings, tendues.

3. feet: crawling foot forward along floor by clenching and relaxing toes, leaving heel on floor

4. tendues parallel forward with flex; brushes

5. dipping foot into 'honey pot', letting honey drip off pointed toe

6. leg swings forward and back 8x right, 4x left, 2x right, 2 claps to finish phrase. Also with sand sack on top of head

7. rising to half toe on both feet slowly and return to flat using image of elevator, possibly starting with demi-plie

Floor

1. shopping: sitting cross-legged in circle, each child reaches for some article (in different directions up, behind, side) while sitting and puts it in the 'basket' formed by legs.
2. boredom: while twirling thumbs slowly roll down from sitting with legs outstretched in front, called back to sitting by wake up call when one quarter, half or two thirds down
3. stockings: sitting with legs outstretched in front run hands down each leg as if taking off stockings, wash stockings, 'hang out to dry' on line high above head. Or: take stockings off w. pointed feet and put back on over flexed feet, using scooping motion with torso (in to up and up over and in)
4. writing name in air with both legs while sitting (balance on bottom)
5. passing objects (keys, etc.) in air with toes to neighbor while sitting (balance on bottom)

Center and through space:

1. low and high steps forward with clapping (either triplets—1 low, 2 high steps or 'family': mother, father, child, child—2 low and 2 high steps)
2. image: apple for space circle using chalk circle, forward and backward (circle in front of dancer or behind)
3. image: spiral staircase for curves
4. more complex locomotive combinations with walks-turns-jumps, w. 3-4 elements and story as motivation (e.g.: cutlery as theme pricking, lifting, cutting, scooping)
5. chassees side alternating (in partners: facing to each other, then away from each other)
6. moving to the sound (percussion instruments)
7. In partners: one is 'musician' using instrument, one dancer. alternating who follows whom
8. finding the jump hidden in the music (individual choice)

8-10 years

A. How they are, developmental pre-conditions, where they're at

I. Physical Elements
a. growth phase continues, at times not proportionally
b. longer concentration span
c. greater memory capacity
d. able to think abstractly
e. more differentiated use of energy

II. Dance Elements
a. enjoy more complex rhythms, spatial paths, varied movement dynamics
b. critical, ambitious, curious
c. whole-body consciousness more developed

III. Improvisation/forming
a. react creatively to suggestions
b. very open
c. enjoy working alone or with others
d. critical, search for criteria

IV. Social Characteristics
a. often 'consciously' socially aware
b. enjoy working with partner of comparable abilities
c. can work well in groups of threes or fours
d. no longer totally uncritical acceptance of teacher
e. uncritical toward self; self-confident

B. Needs, What they like

I. Physical Elements
a. work in space, spatial paths
b. alternating quiet/dynamic phases
c. jumping
d. noticeable progress

II. Dance Elements
a. dynamic, rhythmic, motoric contrasts
b. ambitious movement combinations. more complex jump forms
c. repetitious and repeatable movement patterns

III. Improvisation/forming
a. more ambitious structures, no 'baby' themes, but still imaginative
b. prefer moving with others to solos

c. need clear criteria for observation

d. recognizable contexts

e. assignments with great movement potential

IV. Social Characteristics

a. working with others, especially the 'best friend' or one with comparable abilities,

b. conflict-free environment

c. relate more easily to small group than to entire class

C. Teaching Aims:

I. Physical Elements

a. strengthen back and stomach muscles

b. leg stretches

c. strengthening feet

d. placement

II. Dance Elements

a. make multiple and varied experiences of space possible

b. introduce multiple and varied movement possibilities

c. introduce and utilize clear terminology for movement and dynamics

d. emphasize discipline, standards and respect for art of dance

III. Improvisation/forming

a. emphasize movement, its quality, in movement assignments

b. introduce proper terms in observation phase

c. emphasize beginning-middle-end as form

d. respect students' wishes (themes, music)

e. use teaching aids as introduction to abstraction

IV. Social Characteristics

a. demand and encourage tolerance, cooperation

b. set-up and maintain clear rules of behavior

c. pre-plan group divisions

d. make personal standpoint clear, if necessary, explain reasons

Class activities

Warm-up:

1. running to music, stop on silence, carrying rhythm through in one body part in silence

2. running with mirror—partners run individually, stop when music stops and must mirror the partner without changing the distance between them.

3. negative space: music plays, class runs, on clap 5-6 students make shapes with their body on previously marked spots. Other students, still running to music, plug the spaces in the shape with their body, touching the original person who has made the shape. Original shape resumes running. A new shape is left.

4. on stop, teacher calls out one student's name and one body part. designated student moves named body part, all mirror the movement

5. on stop, teacher gives dynamically defined assignment (like a jellyfish, leaf in wind, cotton ball in water.)

6. all structures involving much movement

Standing Technique (need not be done in circle)

1. Passé

2. swings: arms—forward, side, back; legs—forward and back; body forward and back

3. roll downs with plie in parallel, first and second

4. flat back: spine wave with head leading rolling down to flat back, (head close to body, then leading into flat back) holding arms to side; scooping (head leading down, out and up) in to erect (drop arms)

5. tendues parallel forward and to side turned out

Floor

1. lying on stomach with legs outstretched behind, arms stretched forward and parallel to each other lift arms and legs slowly, sink,—in different combinations (one side both, opposite sides both, only arms, only legs, etc.)

2. lying on back, arms to side bring one leg over the other (spiral) without lifting shoulders

3. lying on back, soles of feet on ground, knees bent parallel and slightly apart, slowly roll up and down spine

4. introduce second position: in sitting, legs apart (knee placement)

5. sitting soles of feet together, knees bent, or legs outstretched in second position, twist torso to right and left, arms held to sides

6. legs outstretched forward, flex and stretch feet, back straight, parallel and turned out.

Center and through space:

1. combinations with 3-5 different elements (e.g. locomotive movement, turn, arm gesture, fall, jump, etc.)

2. combinations with integrated improvisational section

3. combinations with entrances varied spatially and/or in time

4. jump combinations (5 kinds of jumps: from 1 foot to same foot, from 1 foot to the other, from 2 feet to one foot, from 2 feet to 2 feet, from 1 foot to both feet)

5. triangle improvisation—all points of triangle face same way, point person with back to others), moves, others shadow, when point person rotates, all rotate with her, next point person takes over

6. improvisations with, then without teaching aids (e.g. hoops, sticks, cloth, plastic, etc.)

7. require more technical precision in well-known patterns (e.g. skipping combined with "my own treasure chest" s. Curriculum 4-6)

10-12 years

A. How they are: developmental pre-conditions, where they're at
  I. Physical elements
   a. growth phase in full swing, or complete
   b. digital coordination well developed
   c. leg movements not completely controlled, bending, fast steps cause inordinate problems
   d. beginning of puberty
   e. energy level and joy of movement still high
  II. Dance elements
   a. weak arm/leg coordination
   b. do not go to floor as easily as before

c. feet somewhat insensitive due to growth phase

d. can easily remember combinations with 3-4 elements

III. Improvisation/Forming

a. still rather uninhibited

b. curious

c. Understand abstractions, are able to translate into movement

d. understand elements of structure and form and can apply them

IV. Social characteristics

a. loyalty to group is intensified

b. strongly felt sense of fairness with the peer group, but also toward authority figures

c. open to new members of group

B. Needs, what they like

I. Physical elements

a. leaping through space

b. visible progress, improvement

c. alternation of movement-intensive and quiet phases during class.

II. Dance Elements

a. recognizable patterns

b. physical challenges

III. Improvisation/Forming

a. appreciate clear standards, goals

b. enjoy working in groups, do not like to dance alone

c. enjoy creating, forming

IV. Social characteristics

a. friends are more important than the teacher

b. can maintain critical distance to the teacher

C. Teaching Aims: what they should learn

I. Physical elements

a. flexibility & strengthening of torso

b. strengthening foot

c. stretching legs and back

d. increase sensitivity to weighted/non-weighted movement, relaxation

II. Dance Elements

a. increase vocabulary of leg movements

b. make focus more conscious as contrasting element

c. research & name dynamic possibilities

d. strengthen whole-body involvement

e. increase spatial sensitivity

III. Improvisation/Forming

a. increase possibilities of choices in movement and themes, using teaching aids

b. learn to recognize and use compositional forms

IV. Social characteristics

a. learning to accept changes in oneself,—physical, temperamental

b. aid and strengthen sense of group identity

Class Activities

Warm-up

1. Stop & Go. On stop spirals to floor or playing piano w. fingers & toes or swings (body, leg)

2. Meetings: running through space, when you meet another, different tasks (i.e. run around each other, touch certain body part etc)

3. Running with mirror on stops. Partners run individually, stop when music stops and must mirror the partner without changing the distance between them.

Technique

standing:

1. roll downs, flat back with and without arms, release drop torso, roll up

Floor:

1. 1/4 and 1/2 torso circles in first position (soles of feet together, knees apart) with and without arms over head

2. lying on back, pelvis against wall, legs straight up wall (flat back preparation)

3. horizontal arm swings (spirals)

4. lifting nose and sacrum to ceiling (chest lift)

standing:

> 1. tendues, with and without weight transfer, forward, side, back
>
> 2. releves with plies, accelerating into jumps
>
> 3. leg swings, forward, side and figure eights
>
> 4. leg swings with partner holding 2 hands as mirror image
>
> 5. leg swings holding 1 hand with partner, both same leg
>
> 6. leg kicks on floor, then standing
>
> 7. passees parallel & turned out
>
> 8. brushes

Center & through space

1. teach movement combination, each one can revise to suit herself (like 'little black dress'), show in groups to class (not solo).
2. teach assorted unconnected movements. Sort class into groups. Each group assembles their combination together, using all given movements, as they choose. Thematic suggestions can be used, e.g. complete a given spatial path; use given text or picture as mood definer; incorporate textiles or objects.

12-14 Years

A. How they are; developmental pre-conditions; where they're at
   I. Physical elements
      a. deep puberty
      b. often tired, enervated
      c. strong growth phase, possible weight gain
   II. Dance elements
      a. slightly uncoordinated (growth)
      b. appreciate humor rather than seriousness
   III. Improvisation/forming
      a. able to abstract
      b. appreciate clear forms
      c. alternate between adult and childish themes
   IV. Social elements
      a. strong orientation to group
      b. much sympathy, empathy

c. fear of individualized behavior
d. little self-confidence
e. critical

B. Needs; what they like
I. Physical elements
a. clear forms
b. recognizable goals
c. experiencing progress
d. sensitivity training
II. Dance elements
a. acceptable clear goals
b. physically exhausting activities
III. Improvisation/forming
a. clearly structured cooperation
b. self-expression
c. optical effects
IV. Social elements
a. working in groups
b. achievement-oriented
c. honesty

C. Teaching aims; what they should learn
I. Physical elements
a. full physical presence
b. torso stretches
c. foot strengthening
d. enlarged movement vocabulary, e.g. turns, spirals, leg gesture, arm-leg coordination
II. Dance elements
a. longer movement sequences
b. varied spatial orientation (change of fronts)
c. unusual rhythmic patterns
III. Improvisation/forming
a. encourage variety of movement
b. demonstration of alternative (aesthetic) values
c. develop ability for formal and substantive analysis of movement tasks (compositional/choreographic vocabulary)

IV. Social elements
    a. non-confrontational dissolution of cliques
    b. increase self-confidence, self-respect

Class Activities

Warm-up

Alternative 1:
Students lie on floor, scattered through room. Quiet music
Try to bring all body parts into contact with floor, first slowly, then with increasing tempo. Grow slowly up from the floor and sink back. Rise, thinking that the air can be pushed by body parts. Move through the space as you moved on floor, sink to floor, rise, remain standing with eyes closed. When all are standing, fade music. Feel bones, try to stand only on your bones. Let heels rise and sink, open eyes, let heels rise again and sink. What was easier, open or closed?
Alternative 2:
Using energetic music with clear meter: walk through the room, double tempo, half tempo, with large steps on slow tempo, small steps on fast, use arms on slow tempo. Later each plays with rhythm instead of just walking on meter, using arms, and anything else, freeze in motion when and for how long you want to. Resume.

Technique:

standing:
    1. roll downs with plie at bottom, plie releve when erect
    2. flat back, arms in second, w. plie
    3. scooping spine,—in to flat back, out to straight
    4. leg swings forward, side, figure 8
    5. arm swings figure 8, try legs & arms
    6. foot sequence w. front changes: ankle circles, inching foot forward, brush plie/releve, 4 jumps in square w. front change on 4th. Repeat 3 times, so that front changes in quarters.
    7. tendue with & w/o plie, forward. side, back with improv phase between sides, changing front and place in room
    8. brushes into lunge forward and side, with arms, without torso
Floor:
    1. stretches with foot soles together, open position and straight legs forward.

2. rolling up and down spine.

3. chest lift or rolling up and down spine with soles of feet on floor.

4. relaxed, knees near chest, hands on kneecaps, roll from side to side, onto hands and knees

5. on hands and knees, rounding and relaxing spine (hills and valleys), put soles of feet on floor straighten knees (tent) roll up to standing

post floor:

1. triplets forward and backward

2. start battements with brushes, first only forward

3. jumps in place

Improv/Combi

Remind how class started, with experiment going to floor and rising, moving somewhere else and repeating

Teach combi to 6/8, fast 3/4 with locomotive steps, turns or curves, jumps through space, gesture, lasting 4 measures. In partners, both do combi as given. At end using same amount of time, do own sinking to floor and rising. Variation: start combi when partner starts her sink; start from different places in room, with different directions.

14-16 years

A. How they are; developmental pre-conditions; where they're at

   I. Physical elements

      a. almost fully grown

      b. often exhausted, little energy

   II. Dance elements

      a. leave the vertical with great reluctance

      b. whole-body coordination lacking occasionally

      c. often adapt role model postures

   III. Improvisation/forming

      a. enjoy clear themes, forms

      b. do not enjoy working alone

      c. no longer so open, uncritical

   V. Social elements

      a. are fairly unsure of themselves

      b. very dependent on group

      c. fairly critical of teacher, each other, themselves

B. Needs; what they like
  I. Physical elements
      a. relaxation
      b. achievable requirements
  II. Dance elements
      a. strongly rhythmical sequences
      b. recognizable forms
      c. short-term goals
      d. recognizable progress
  III. Improvisation/forming
      a. prefer abstract themes to real-life ones
      b. resort often to pop dance formations (MTV)
      c. enjoy dancing with props, objects
  V. Social elements
      a. clear standards of behavior
      b. fairness
      c. substantive criticism

C. Teaching aims; what they should learn
  I. Physical elements
      a. mobilization of energy
      b. presentation of alternative postures
      c. strengthening torso
  II. Dance elements
      a. stretching legs, back, feet
      b. enlarge movement vocabulary, precise terminology
      c. refine dynamic possibilities
      d. present aesthetic alternatives
  III. Improvisation/forming
      a. make dance as art form more available through videos, photos, etc.
      b. introduce compositional forms
      c. intensify reflective phases, related to re-working, repeating
  V. Social elements
      a. strengthen self-confidence
      b. dissolve cliques
      c. enforce tolerance

Class Activities

Warm-up
scatter various objects throughout space, e.g. rope, stick, pail, chair, hat, umbrella, plastic bag, one object more than number of students. Use melodic music. Students should dance with object, trying out what's possible, or move like object, or the opposite. Change objects at will.

Technique
everything from before, plus, with experienced students:

> swing plies with arms and torso change
> brush lunges with torso change
> body swings with front changes
> jumps in place w. 1/4 and 1/2 turns
> jumps through space with off-center torso
> spiral turns
> leg swings figure 8 with arms and contract-release

Improv/combi
Using photo, painting or text: confusing? peaceful? exciting? aggressive? fast? slow? sad? lonely? How can the movement express this?

Each student develops a movement chain including locomotive movement, turns, jumps and going to floor (and rising) with beginning and end 5 meters apart. Teach it to a partner and learn hers. Mix the two, paying attention to organic transitions.

16-18 Years

A. How they are; developmental pre-conditions; where they're at
Although youngsters at this age appear to be like adults (and often are), they can feel under-challenged in adult classes, even though technically they can barely keep up. They have high expectations and need new challenges. Adults are happy when they can get to class. Young people demand more, want to be totally absorbed, to lose themselves in the movement.

The teacher (here no longer a contact person but rather an expert in her field or a role model) can, commensurate with the students' dance experience, present a class with greater variety and more creative work than in a class for adults.

I. Physical elements
    a. growth phase complete

b. weight problems, anorexia, bulimia, can appear or become more serious

II. Dance elements
like adults

III. Improvisation/forming
a. can deal with abstractions
b. can deal with emotions as a theme
c. enjoy working on longer forms and/or projects

IV. Social elements
a. attachment to group remains strong
b. able to exercise tolerance
c. start to develop political and social conscience
d. often try out non-conformist attitudes, opinions or dress

B. Needs; what they like
I. Physical elements
a. variety
b. to push to physical limits

II. Dance elements
a. diversity
b. recognizable achievement

III. Improvisation/forming
a. acceptable themes (not too childish)
b. assignments with strong movement potential

IV. Social elements
To be taken seriously

C. Teaching aims; what they should learn

I. Physical elements

a. counteract movement habits

>use floor stretches, floor combinations often
>give beginners exact corrections and the reasons for them
>demand more precision, do not overlook mistakes, maintain standards
> use the mirror as an aid, but do not always work facing mirror
> change front for class by moving teaching position

b. increase physical and mental flexibility

> use energetic or very clear warm-up structure. Not too compli-
cated
> use varied styles of music (perhaps not in one class)
> change often between work in small groups, with whole class,
solo and group improvisation

II. Dance elements

a. broaden and refine movement vocabulary

> if possible change and identify dance styles
> work longer and more exactly on technique, do not overlook mis-
takes
> work technical exercises in partners facing each other, in order to
avoid mask-like expressions

III. Improvisation/forming

a. provide appropriate forms for work on emotional themes

b. increase knowledge and use of compositional tools

> follow reflection phase with action phase, incorporating comments
if possible
> if possible use innovative/newer improvisational techniques (e.g.
chance, contact)

IV. Social elements

like adults

APPENDIX B

Lifesavers for a bad dance day

When you have a "bad dance day"

All of us have days when teaching dance seems foreign, challenging, impossible. In my experience there are two kinds of "bad dance day".

The first is when you have no ideas. The plans you made the night before or on the weekend seem impractical and uninteresting. You're tired,—in general, but also of dancing, of teaching, of children and young people. Of course, being a professional, you get there, and when you're there, you do it as best you can.

It helps to have resources for this kind of situation. It could be the use of your favorite music, even if it's not "child-friendly". Your response to it will help bridge your personal credibility gap. The same is true for a prop—a favorite skirt or hat, for example—that has a meaning for you, a memory or maybe just your own interest in how it moves, what images it stirs; or a story that you are particularly fond of, a book, a picture. Anything which touches you personally, immediately will be more effective than trying yet again to go the usual route,—what's my lesson goal? what did we do last week? what to continue? what new things to introduce? Whatever the reason, that route has proven momentarily unfruitful for you. It's time to try another. (It may be a welcome change for the class, too.) As you have chosen your profession, hopefully, because you love it, it helps to go back to what you love, at least this one time, rather than what you think is good for the class. Trust your instincts and your enthusiasm. That interest and enthusiasm will communicate itself to the class.

The second sort of "bad dance day" can happen when there is some sort of trauma in your personal life. Teaching can sometimes provide an island of sanity, a place to finally get your mind off of the illness, the divorce, the child-rearing problems. But there are times when you feel alienated from your students, from dance and even from yourself. These times, when you seem to be standing beside yourself, when you can hear yourself speaking, when you are estranged, are very threatening. They are also very subjective, and that must be remembered. I have often come out of class depressed by my disconnection, only to hear from colleagues that it was a particularly good class. Many teachers have experienced this, not just dance teachers.

I think that dance offers more opportunities to surmount this barrier. Movement connects you back to yourself. This is true for the students as well as for the teacher. Improvising with the class, or moving with them (not in front of them) through the room in a combination, gives you the chance to realize yourself as a dancer, not just a teacher, to connect back to yourself. If that doesn't help do something completely different like a whole hour on group interaction and group dynamics, using 'blind games'.

One game my classes always loved was Labyrinth: one person volunteers to be 'blind'. She faces the wall while the rest of the class makes a labyrinth out of their bodies, each one connecting to the next and deciding on the "proper" way through, if the 'blind' one must go over the legs, under the arms etc. This must be done in silence, otherwise she knows what's happening. The group decides on a positive and negative noise to lure her in the right path or to warn her when she is going off course, e.g. hissing for a warning and clicking with the tongue as a lure. When the labyrinth is done, the teacher puts the blindfold on the girl, brings her to the beginning of the labyrinth and the fun starts. Besides being fun, labyrinth enforces group action. Only one person can make the lure sound, otherwise the blind one is confused. The group must act together to get the blind one through. And there is no talking, which enforces concentration. About three students can be 'blind' before the class gets tired of this. (In a class of 12, getting through the labyrinth can take 8—10 minutes for each labyrinth). A new labyrinth is formed for each 'blind' student. There are many other useful and amusing games like this. It pays to have a few of them up the sleeve of your leotard.

Another completely different approach is drawing to music. Roll out paper rolls, or use old posters or used flip chart paper and let the students draw to the music with felt pens. Encourage them to make the music visible, not draw horses, houses and flowers on a mini scale. Classical music is nice for this, the French composers Debussy etc. or Dvorjak, or opera overtures. After a certain time drawing their own pictures, let them put away the pens and dance what they have drawn, again to the music. Point out the sharp angles, circles and remind them that these should be seen in their bodies too when they dance the drawing. Then let them change places, using someone else's drawing to "dance to".

A film or video about dance or dancers may be old stuff to you, but to your students this is exotic. Discussing it afterwards with the students gives them more insights about dance and about you, just as you learn about them from their comments. The discussion is very important. See if they understand the dance, what it was about, if it was interesting for them and why. The same effect can be had from a dance book if a video or VCR is not available.

Another more physical solution is letting them choose poses from the photos in a dance book, making them fit to their bodies (doing a split with the arms instead of the legs for example) then letting them make trios going from pose to pose, or try as many ways as possible to get into the pose and to leave it. You can slip in a little dance history on the way, telling them the background of this dancer or that choreographer.

If you have the time to arrange it, having a guest come to class is always interesting. An actor, a mime, or a flamenco dancer can show a bit and do very simple things with the class.

Or arrange a trip to a performance or to a rehearsal of professional dancers.

Or let contiguous classes do one thing together before the first class leaves. This is especially effective when there's an age difference between the classes.

If these sound interesting, file them away. Don't use them needlessly. The novelty is part of the value. Like the money my mother always saved for a rainy day, it's nice to have them when you need them,—when you've misplaced the invitation, when there's absolutely no dance left in your head.

APPENDIX C

Stories to dance to

Dancing Stories

For the 4-6 year olds even a 60-minute class can seem long. 6-8 year olds, already tired from the school day, lose concentration. For these children, dancing a story can make the end of class into a new adventure.

If you have a lively imagination, you can ask the children to name three things that should be in the story. It's wise to avoid well-known figures from other stories—and no princesses. The trick is to catch their attention right at the beginning by suggesting outlandish objects, for example a frying pan or a rubber boot. Giving human qualities to inanimate objects gives you the chance to create unusual movement. Use as much space as you can, different levels and directions as well as varied movement qualities (dynamics). Everyone, including you, dances the story as you tell it. Don't stop the flow of either the movement or the story. The children will watch you for movement clues. Don't let them stop moving to listen. The movement is more important than the story!

Reading children's books and fairy tales again will give you a good feeling for how these stories are built. There is always—like in a dance!—a beginning: dance the present state of the object. The middle is usually a conflict or a change. This can be as complex and long as you want. In the following story it's the screw's voyage through the re-cycling bin as well as the imbedding in the boot. The end should be short and sweet. These children are listening and moving on all cylinders and can only do it for a limited time.

I usually start these stories 10 minutes before the end of class when the children have gotten tired and finish in time to do a closing ritual (clapping a farewell in rhythm or the leap across the space and out the door). Remember, a 3-minute dance is long.

It's wiser to limit this to the age groups mentioned above. Older children cannot suspend their disbelief as well and object to the lack of reality. Learning to differentiate between 'true' and 'false', 'right' and 'wrong' in school unfortunately often keeps them from the enthusiastic enjoyment of 'nonsense'.

I always enjoy this, but if you don't, it's better to leave it. You might try it in privacy first to see how it feels.

Here are two stories, one with movement suggestions, one without.

A screwy story

Once upon a time there was a screw.

Make a spiral out of your body. Plant your feet firm on the ground and twist twist twist your body so that you're looking over your shoulder with your arms wrapped around yourself.

It was an old screw and some of its parts didn't work so well anymore. It was hard to screw in.

turn around yourself very slowly

Every time someone tried to use the screw, it got harder and harder to turn.

turn slower and slower

Sometimes it would just get stuck and not turn any further.

try to make your body turn more but don't move your feet: you're stuck!

Sometimes it would go into the wood crooked.

tilt a bit, like a crooked screw.

Even the point at the end was blunt.

turn your feet in toward each other

Finally the screw's owner got angry and tossed the screw out into the garbage, not just the ordinary garbage, but into the recycling bin. The screw, being rather small, slipped and slid down the pile of empty tin cans, plastic jars and rusty cake pans, to land with a tinkle on a flat surface at the bottom of the bin.

Let yourself collapse out of your screw shape and dodge through the space avoiding imaginary tin cans etc. Get lower and lower as you tumble. Let your arms flail a bit and dodge those cake pans with your hips and your tummy too. Land flat on the floor.

At first it thought it had reached the bottom of the bin, but as it looked around it saw that it had landed on a something flat with walls around it. The screw rolled around for a while, trying to see how big the flat thing was.
Roll around on the floor.

He kept bumping into walls.
Bump into imaginary walls and reverse your rolling direction.

Finally he realized that he had landed in a frying pan. He looked up to see why the pan was empty. Above his head was a big bag full of Styrofoam chips that made it impossible for larger things to slide past. He tried to push at it, but it was too far away.

The screw had the pan all to himself.
Lying on your back on the floor, push above you with your arms and legs, really try to reach that imaginary plastic bag, but leave your back on the floor.

He rolled around trying to get a grip on his surroundings, when suddenly his whole world tilted to the right, then to the left, then back again. The screw was thrown against the walls and floor of the pan. Wherever he landed he made noise.

He rolled around, trying to get a grip on his surroundings, when suddenly his whole world tilted to the right, then to the left, then back again. Sometimes it was a tinkle, sometimes a slap, sometimes he made more than one sound as first his head then his blunt old foot hit the metal pan.
Stretch out one foot in some direction, then your other foot in another direction, then an arm. You can use your head or your bottom or your elbow or your hip. Try to make a sound when you reach that imaginary pan.

The screw liked the sounds he made, but when he tried to make them again, it didn't work. Suddenly everything started to shake.
That's right—start to shake—your whole entire body. As you shake let that bring you up to standing (Your hands can do some shaking and your head. A little is good for the brain!).

The screw vibrated, making really fast sounds against the pan. "Holy Smoke!" he thought, "What's going on here?" The shaking continued, and in addition, everything started to tilt.

Everything in the bin started sliding. The screw passed the tins, bottles and pans and lots of other things he couldn't even name, everything was turning and twisting and tumbling.

Now's the time to really shake, rattle and roll around your space. End with a final shake and freeze.

Finally, after a particularly violent shake, the screw rolled away from all the other things in the bin and landed in a puddle in the gutter.

Turn slowly away to another place, stop and shiver.

The screw was definitely not comfortable. He shivered and shook in the wet cold and thought longingly of the wonderful sounds he had made in the nice dry frying pan.

Cars drove by, splashing him. Kids jumped over his puddle, their rubber boots flying over his head. He was feeling very sad. As he looked up, waiting for the next pair of flying boots, he saw one rubber boot descending right on him.

Look up, get frightened, and shrink slowly down as if something's pushing you.

The next thing he knew, he was imbedded in the rubber sole of a bright red right boot, size 6 1/2.

Slowly come back to your real size as if you're pushing your way up into the space.

The red boot, and its mate, the left boot, clumped along carrying the screw down the street and into a place that had a stone floor.

Jump 4 or 5 times from 2 feet to 2 feet (like a rabbit) to another place, landing heavily on the last jump.

The screw knew this, and so did the boot, and so did the boot's owner because that screw was making a very loud noise!

The owner scraped the boot along the floor, hoping to get rid of the noise. She stamped, dragged, flopped that boot around, but the screw stayed put.

Drag one foot after you, jump and hop around.

He was having a wonderful time making all the wonderful sounds he remembered from the frying pan adventure. After a while, the owner looked at the boot's sole and realized it was hopeless.

Lie down and put your feet in the air—as if you were upside down.

If she pulled out the screw there would be a hole in her boot. If she left the screw in, it would at least keep the hole closed. She decided to make the best of a bad situation. She danced around the railroad station (that's where the stone floor was), making all kinds of wonderful sounds.
Hop, skip and jump around the space.

As she was only 10, many people stopped to look. On the spot her parents decided to give her tap dancing lessons. She became a famous dancer later, but she always kept the boot with her for luck. The screw was in seventh heaven, surrounded constantly with all the wonderful sounds he had first heard in the frying pan. The boot was happy because he was the only rubber boot to make it as a tap dancer!
Take a bow!

Halloween, the Hippie and the wristwatch
The watch ticked and ticked. Tick, tick, tick went the small hand, working as hard as it could. Minute by minute it got closer and closer to the big hand. "This time it will work. I know it will," thought the small hand to himself. As he came up to the big hand he pushed and pushed but he could not budge the big hand. The big hand just stuck there, pointing calmly at the number 11.
Suddenly the watch tilted as its owner, Harry the Hippie, looked at the time. "Oh good!" he thought. "Lots of time. I can go back to sleep." The watch tipped back to flat.
Just as the small hand was about to start pushing again, something started to shake the watch. It shook and rattled and swung back and forth. Harry the Hippie had never done anything like this before. In fact, where was Harry? There was no long sleeve covering the face of the watch, no long hair tickling it. The watch flew through air as if thrown by invisible hands, and in between every flight was a shake and a rattle.
Finally the movement stopped. It started to get very cold. Both hands started to shiver. The numbers on the watch face shivered. All the little cogs and wheels and gears inside the watch started to shiver. They shivered so much that they got mixed up. The hands were inside where the wheels used to be, the cogs were on the watch face were the numbers used to be, everything was just at sixes and sevens. The small hand crept over to the big hand and hid himself underneath.

"This is all your fault," he whispered. "You're supposed to push me around the clock, you dummy! That's why we lost the tock and just ticked."

"Ssshhh. I got tired. You think it's fun pushing all day and night? If Harry the Hippie can get away without working so can I!" All the cogs and wheels and numbers nodded and said "me too".

Suddenly, all the wristwatch parts heard a deep gong, then another and another and another—12 gongs! It was midnight.

All the watch parts froze. The small hand tried to become even smaller. "Now you've done it.," he whispered. "While you were all being lazy, Halloween started and Harry will miss the party because he doesn't know what time it is."

"Oh yes he will. He'll know the time.," a ghostly voice said. In the darkness a small white glob became brighter and brighter. Soon, instead of being just a small glob it had a head and body and arms and legs and a face and freckles and very long, messy hair. "Just watch this!"

The white body began to poke at Harry the Hippie, it tickled his feet and pulled his hair and blew in his face. Harry brushed away the ghostly hands and kept right on sleeping. The small white body stamped its feet and waved his arms. Then it took a deep breath and got bigger and bigger until it was enormous. In a deep, deep voice it said "Harry, wake up! It's me, your ghost. I've had enough of you lying about." Harry woke up and looked around. When he saw the ghost he tried to hide under the blanket. The ghost whipped off the blanket. Harry jumped under the bed. The ghost crawled under the bed. Harry ran to the window. The ghost grabbed his shoulder and spun him around just as he was about to climb out. "Oh no you don't. You just sit right there" and the ghost sat Harry down hard in a chair.

A cold, ghostly hand passed over Harry's head. His long hair was gone. A cold wind passed over his whole body. His wonderful old, comfortable, ragged clothes were gone. Harry was wearing a suit and a tie and had very short hair!

Harry felt a tickle on his wrist. He looked down and saw his wristwatch. He held it up to his ear and heard "tick tock tick tock". The big hand was moving around a lot. The small hand was moving very, very slowly toward one. The cogs and wheels were nowhere to be seen and the numbers were right there where they were supposed to be.

"Now you can go to the Halloween party," said the ghostly voice.

Harry was nervous and upset. He knew all his friends would laugh at him. No one would believe that Harry the Hippie had turned into a businessman for Halloween. Maybe they wouldn't even recognize him! He tried to unbutton the jacket. It didn't work. He threw himself onto the bed and writhed and twisted and turned, trying to get out of the awful suit. He pumped with his legs and twisted his arms, and stretched in all directions. It got very warm. He was having trouble breathing. He started to cough and suddenly it got very light. Harry tried to look around, but there was something covering his eyes. It was his hair! It had come back. Harry looked down and saw his wonderful old clothes. They were back. It was all a dream, just a terrible nightmare. Then he looked down at his wristwatch, tick, tocking away. Tick Tock Tick Tock! Wow, thought Harry. Maybe it was real after all. At any rate, it was time to go the party. As Harry walked out the door, a small white blob followed him, watching Harry's wrist carefully. The small hand and the big hand peered up at the white blob. No more goofing off, the big hand thought, no more coming late, just tick tocking around the clock, except maybe … next Halloween …

Bibliography

Teaching

"Movement and Dance in Early Childhood", Mollie Davies. Paul Chapman Publishing, London, 2003

"Creative Dance for all Ages", Anne Green Gilbert. The American Alliance for Health, Physical Education, Recreation and Dance, AAHPERD, Reston, Va., 1992

"Human Movement Potential", Lulu Sweigard. Harper and Row, 1974

"Brain-Compatible Dance Education", Anne Green Gilbert. National Dance Association/AAHPERD 2006

"In Touch with Dance", Marion Gough, Whitethorn Books, Lancaster, 1993

Choreography

"The Intimate Art of Choreography", Lynn Anne Blom, L. Tarin Chaplin. University of Pittsburgh Press, 1982

"The Mary Wigman Book" Walter Sorell, Wesleyan University Press, 1973

"Reading Dancing", Susan Leigh Foster. University of California Press, Berkley, Los Angeles, London, 1986

Improvisation

"Dance Improvisations", Joyce Morgenroth, University of Pittsburgh Press, Pittsburgh, PA., 1987

"Improvisation for the Theater", Viola Spolin, Northwestern University Press, 1963

"Body Space Image", Miranda Tufnell and Chris Crickmay, Dance Books, 1990

"The Moment of Movement" Lynn Anne Blom, L. Tarin Chaplin. University of Pittsburgh Press, 1988

Dance History

"No Fixed Points, Dance in the Twentieth Century", Nancy Reynolds and Malcolm McCormick. Yale University Press, New Haven 2003

"The Makers of Modern Dance in Germany", Isa Partsch-Bergsohn & Harold Bergsohn, Princeton Books 2003

"Hitler's Dancers", Lilian Karina, Marion Kant. Berghahn Books, 2003

"Terpsichore in Sneakers", Sally Banes. Wesleyan University Press 1977

"Time and the Dancing Image", Deborah Jowitt. University of California Press, Berkeley and Los Angeles, 1988

"Liebe Hanya, Mary Wigman's Letters to Hanya Holm"" Claudia Gitelman, University of Wisconsin Press 2003

For school teachers

"Math Dance", Karl Schaeffer, Erik Stern, Scott Kim, schafferkarl"@fhda.edu, estern@weber.edu, 2001

"Teaching The Three Rs Through Movement", Anne Green Gilbert. National Dance Education Organization, contact info@ndao.org

978-0-595-47253-6
0-595-47253-2

www.ingramcontent.com/pod-product-compliance
Lightning Source LLC
Chambersburg PA
CBHW051247050326
40689CB00007B/1104